1 MONTH OF FREE READING

at

www.ForgottenBooks.com

By purchasing this book you are eligible for one month membership to ForgottenBooks.com, giving you unlimited access to our entire collection of over 1,000,000 titles via our web site and mobile apps.

To claim your free month visit:

www.forgottenbooks.com/free82195

* Offer is valid for 45 days from date of purchase. Terms and conditions apply.

ISBN 978-0-266-97170-2
PIBN 10082195

This book is a reproduction of an important historical work. Forgotten Books uses state-of-the-art technology to digitally reconstruct the work, preserving the original format whilst repairing imperfections present in the aged copy. In rare cases, an imperfection in the original, such as a blemish or missing page, may be replicated in our edition. We do, however, repair the vast majority of imperfections successfully; any imperfections that remain are intentionally left to preserve the state of such historical works.

Forgotten Books is a registered trademark of FB &c Ltd.
Copyright © 2018 FB &c Ltd.
FB &c Ltd, Dalton House, 60 Windsor Avenue, London, SW19 2RR.
Company number 08720141. Registered in England and Wales.

For support please visit www.forgottenbooks.com

THE BRITISH COAL INDUSTRY

BY
GILBERT STONE
BARRISTER-AT-LAW
SOMETIME DEPUTY HEAD OF PRODUCTION COAL MINES
DEPARTMENT, ASSISTANT SECRETARY COAL INDUSTRY
COMMISSION, AND SECRETARY TO THE
CONTROLLERS' ADVISORY BOARD

1919
LONDON & TORONTO
J. M. DENT & SONS, LTD.
NEW YORK: E. P. DUTTON & CO.

HD9551
.5
S7

All rights reserved.

PREFACE

AT a recent conference at the Coal Mines' Department the Right Honourable William Brace, M.P., the South Wales miners' leader and lately Under Secretary for Home Affairs, used the following words: "The real dying need of the world in general, and of this nation in particular at this moment, is production." This sentence may form the text of this book which is not concerned to support this or that theory of management, and does not adventure into technical details, but is intended to place before the reader well-ascertained facts from which he may form his own conclusions as to the financial and industrial future of this country if present conditions relative to this industry do not improve.

It is probable that, even as in the past so also in the future, this country will surmount all difficulties and win her way through her present trials. It is not to be expected, however, that the numerous grave and perplexing troubles of to-day will be overcome if we merely throw up our hands in despair. Nor shall we accomplish anything of service by burying our heads in the sand, ostrich-like, and refusing to see. We must see and we must act or the war that is won will be lost.

Knowing as I do most of the leaders on both the coal owners' and the miners' side, and entertaining for them the highest regard, it is to me very regrettable to have perpetually to refer to the shortcomings of the industry. This, however, seems to be unavoidable when we have to deal with an industry which is at present the battling-ground for a great and fundamental change.

To quote a particular instance we have seen this industry held up to public criticism on account of the housing of its workers. Deplorable conditions have been shown to exist in some cases. This has earned the industry a bad name in many quarters. Yet, if we look at the matter fairly, should we not say that this is an evil no more peculiar to the coal industry than to any other? Have we not our slums? That such things should be is indefensible and every effort is being made to-day to abolish this last remnant of a by-gone age, but they show that the coal owners are in no worse case than the generality of those responsible for the housing of the working classes.

We say this as a prelude to asking the reader not to approach the question from the point of view either that the owners are tyrants or that the miners' leaders are revolutionaries of the Bolshevik type. It simply is not so. Throughout the war, when the very fate of our country depended in no slight measure upon the proper working of our

PREFACE

mines, both master and miner and miners' leader made stupendous efforts to cope with the immense difficulties which lack of man-power, lack of material and war nerves created.

There is, indeed, underlying the present coal situation, a deep psychological and sociological problem which, though it has manifested itself in relation to this industry, is in existence equally in the case of other industries. Upon the solution of this problem depends the existence or elimination of the present system whereby capital employs labour. It is obvious that we have here one of the Grand Disputes, full of combustible material, full of intellectual difficulties, full of importance, pregnant with possibilities and impossibilities.

Yet though this is so, though we have reached perhaps one of the turning-points in the industrial history of our country, we must realize that of those who will have the decision in the last resort only a very small fraction have any clear idea either of the problem or the industry.

In such circumstances it is always desirable to sweep away personalities and permit facts to take the place of prejudices. This is the second purpose of this book.

As the problem is so largely a psychological and so little a material one, I have, after much consideration, decided to include two short chapters on the history of the industry. My doubt as to the propriety of this course was due to the fact that the past history of the coal trade shows many grave abuses and many wrongs committed against defenceless labour—male, female and child—and I doubted whether the mere recounting of past wrongs might not increase the tension between employer and employed. My decision was taken because it appeared to me that it must be obvious that times have completely changed, and that it is greatly to the credit of the present and the immediately preceding generation of owners and mine managers, as well as to the Trade Unions concerned, that the intolerable conditions of 1842 have been so completely swept away.

The various views expressed by me in the course of this book express my personal opinion only and are in no way official.

I desire to express my thanks to Mr. W. L. Cook for kindly reading the last chapter and making suggestions relative to inclusive and exclusive price lists.

GILBERT STONE.

INNER TEMPLE,
  LONDON.

CONTENTS

CHAPTER		PAGE
I.	Early Days	1
II.	Later Legislation	33
III.	The Working of a Modern Colliery	50
IV.	Output	73
V.	Enquiries and Experiences	100
VI.	The Export Trade	121
VII.	The Home Consumer	142
VIII.	Wages and Disputes	164
	Index	185

THE BRITISH COAL INDUSTRY

CHAPTER I

EARLY DAYS

ARISTOTLE once adventured the opinion that things with which the political science is conversant possess so great an ambiguity that we must be satisfied if we can indicate the truth by a rude adumbration and if our conclusions are similar in accuracy to the things themselves.

There is certainly so great a diversity in the points of view from which the facts pertaining to the present conditions of the coal industry may be viewed as to make both the presentation of these facts and the deducing of conclusions therefrom a matter of singular difficulty so that men equally endowed may arrive at conclusions the most diverse. It is so largely a matter of the point of view, and that depends hardly so much upon reason as upon sentiment.

This being the state of our case, it is not impertinent to enquire before plunging *in medias res* somewhat into the history of the industry, so that we may encounter wrongs long dead but still living in memory and affecting viewpoint, so that we may obtain 'atmosphere,' and see something of the way in which the industry has developed and of the conditions under which it has been carried on.

Within recent years the status of the industry and its workers has entirely changed. From being the Cinderella of Labour it has become the Princess, and its leaders now speak on equal terms with Ministers instead of being ordered by magistrates to go back to their homes peaceably and not trouble the august personages in London, as were the demonstrators who dragged their loads of coal to the Metropolis in the hope of laying their woes before the Prince Regent during the distress which followed on the Signing of Peace in 1815. To-day many of the owners of coal-mines are in the forefront of the business world. Several, like the late Lord Rhondda, have stamped their name on the history of the country. To-day colliery management is a subject of high technicality requiring long training and much specialized knowledge. A hundred years ago matters were very different. A few great names stand out from a throng of persons who were mediocre, conservative and slow. Yet even in the early days of the industry there were, as we shall see, constant efforts being made to improve the technical conditions of coal-mining. Surveying the history of our subject as a whole we can say that it shows a constant though slow upward tendency on the technical side and, at least up to the time of Lord Ashley's Bill of 1842, a drab monotony of toil on the labour side.

Already, by the end of the thirteenth century, coal was being got or mined on the Tyne and in South Yorkshire, Derbyshire, Nottinghamshire, Shropshire, the Forest of Dean, Staffordshire, Lancashire, North and South Wales and Scotland. At that period, of course, it was not used as a fuel for household purposes but almost exclusively by lime-burners and smiths, though the salters also occasionally evaporated their brine-water by its means.

The first attempt to use it as a fuel was the cause of a revolt in London in 1306, and the brewers and dyers who were mainly responsible for the nuisance were compelled to return to the use of charcoal. It was not until about 1570 that coal came into common use for household purposes, not, indeed, until the invention of the chimney had abolished the black clouds of smoke such as had driven Queen Eleanor from her apartments at Nottingham. Its employment for smelting did not become general until the early part of the eighteenth century.

It was with the extended use of coal that the industry first began to shed its swaddling clothes. But already so many of the major peculiarities of the trade, as a mystery, had been developed that it is necessary shortly to describe their development during the fourteenth and fifteenth centuries.

To-day it is not unknown for a coal-mine to be 3000 ft. deep and to extend for many miles underground. The method of working is almost invariably either by bord and pillar, or longwall, both of which we shall shortly describe hereafter. To-day it is comparatively rare for an explosion to occur, and when it does occur the damage caused is slight, or is caused by the ignition of the explosive mixture formed by fine coal-dust floating in air. To-day it is common for thousands of gallons of water to be pumped thousands of feet every minute and for great ventilating fans to create a current of air in the workings below which renders the air, in the normal case and apart from 'blows' of fire-damp, little more unhealthy or dangerous than the air in an ordinary open cavern. To-day it is necessary for mining engineers to deal with many nice problems relating to support and boundaries. Subsidences, drainage, trespass, all have to be considered. In the age of which we now speak it was very different, but already these fundamental difficulties of the industry were presenting themselves and were beginning to be solved.

The first form of pit was the Bell pits. The miner working on an outcrop—that is to say, on a coal seam which by geological action has been thrown upwards or has been disclosed so that the coal breaks out from the surface of the earth—dug a circular hole a few feet in diameter and then proceeded to dig round a few feet beneath the surface until the hole in section presented a bell-shaped figure. The coal thus got was hauled up in a basket, and the mine when exhausted was abandoned and a new hole made a few yards away.

These very primitive mines were only possible in cases of a true outcrop. It soon became necessary to follow the seam to a lower depth, and immediately the difficulty of drainage presented itself. Thereupon these early miners developed the aqueduct or adit system of working—a method which is still practised in some very small and shallow mines to-day.

We find in the lease granted in 1364 by Bishop Hatfield to burgesses of Newcastle and Gateshead, the first reference clearly indicative of the fact that mining was then being done by means of pits and adits, or water-gates as they were then called. The method was simple and effective where the mining was being conducted above the level of free drainage, but was impossible otherwise. It consisted in sinking a shaft on to the seam, which would be known from the outcrop, and then working up the seam towards the outcrop, at the same time cutting a tunnel or adit from the shaft rather more than at right angles to it and continuing the shaft until the outside air was reached. The water was then simply drained away and all the many difficulties connected with flooding were eliminated.

The adit system of drainage entirely depended, however, on the working being above the level of free drainage. Thus, in the figure shown, it was impossible under this system to work down the seam, for then the water would flow on to the workings. It was consequently early found necessary to supplement this natural mode of drainage by the artificial raising of water, and as early as 1486 the sum of £9 15s. 6d. occurs in the accounts of the Finchale monks in respect of the cost of setting up a pump which was probably of the wheel and bucket type worked by horses.

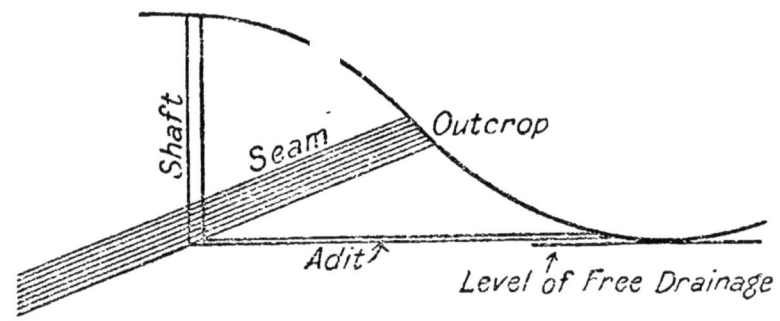

These or similar simple methods of drainage were the only ones available for centuries until, indeed, the invention of the steam engine in the eighteenth century rendered it possible to lift water for almost an unlimited height and at a great rate. As a result many of the early mines were, in a short time, drowned out and had to be abandoned. Many attempts to overcome this difficulty were made, notably that of Captain Savery, whose steam suction plant for pumping water was patented in 1698. All failed, however, owing to the fact that the power obtainable was

EARLY DAYS

too low to obtain the necessary lift. The first steam engine for raising water was the invention of Newcomen, an ironmonger of Southampton, and was laid down with the help of Savery at a Staffordshire pit in 1712, when, in two lifts, the water was raised to a height of 153 ft. By 1716 the 'fire-engine' pump had been established at a large number of mines and one of the great problems of mining was in a fair way to be solved.[1]

The second great difficulty of mining—explosions—was not experienced to any considerable extent in the early days of the industry owing to the smallness and shallowness of the mines. The first recorded accident took place in 1378 and was not connected with fire-damp but with water.

It was not, indeed, until the seventeenth century that fire-damp explosions began to present a real obstacle to working, and the first clear account of an explosion is that given by Mostyn in the *Philosophical Transactions* for 1677.[2] It was as the result of this accident, which he there describes, that the first 'fireman' was employed by the colliers in North Wales to go down before them, dressed in rags, to creep along with a lighted candle on the end of a pole and set fire to the 'damp.'

---

[1] Mr. Galloway in his *Annals of Coal Mining* informs us that "previous to the erection of the steam engine, more than fifty horses were employed in raising water at Griff Colliery, at an expense of not less than £900 a year; whereas the annual cost of the engine never exceeded £150."

[2] One of the first recorded explosions took place at Gateshead in 1621.

Thus originated the office of fireman, examiner, or deputy, which exists to-day in full force as we shall see; only to-day the circumstances of the duty have entirely changed and the fireman, instead of being a man who for a pittance is prepared to face death day by day, is now the holder of a position superior to that of the collier, a position of responsibility and of some authority, and one upon whom to no small extent depends the safety of the men at the face.[1]

Once, however, the difficulties connected with deep shaft sinking and drainage had been partially overcome, the greater depth and extent of mines rendered the danger of explosions much greater, and the early years of the eighteenth century were marked by two disasters of considerable magnitude, one at Fat Field, Chester-le-Street, killing no fewer than sixty-nine persons. This pit was 57 fathoms deep, i.e. 342 ft.—an exceptional depth in those days—yet two men and one woman were blown from the bottom up the shaft and a considerable distance into the air.

Fire-damp and other noxious gases have presented and still present some of the most difficult problems which the mining engineer has to face. The main weapon against them is ventilation, though in late years dusting has been found a cure for certain types of explosions. Ventilation there-

---

[1] i.e. the place where the coal is being got—the coal-face. Mine labour is roughly divisible into three parts : (1) Those employed at the face ; (2) those employed on the roads (underground) ; (3) those employed on the surface.

EARLY DAYS

fore, like drainage, is a matter which it is necessary shortly to touch upon in order that the reader may have some idea of the conditions appertaining in a mine.

The miner is faced with two kinds of perils connected with noxious gases—explosion and poisoning. Explosions may be caused by fire-damp, i.e. methane, or by air and coal dust. In the early days of the industry practically all the explosions were due to fire-damp; to-day, though they may be, and generally are, initiated by fire-damp, which disturbs the air and causes the coal dust lying on the haulage roads to rise, the damage resulting is usually caused by coal dust.

Indeed it would be safe to say that more loss of life is due to poisonous than explosive gases to-day. The first medical man to enquire into noxious vapours in mines was Dr. Caius, the great Tudor physician, who, writing in the middle of the sixteenth century, said: " The unwholesome vapours are so pernicious to the hired labourers that they would immediately destroy them if they did not get out of the way as soon as the flame of their lamps becomes blue and is consumed." Here the learned doctor is probably speaking of fire-damp, a colourless odourless gas which exists in coal seams usually at a high pressure sometimes as great as 400 lb. to the square inch. This gas is only about half the weight of air, burns with a bluish flame and, in conjunction with air, forms a mixture which will explode when brought into contact with a naked light or even a spark. In the words of Dr. Shufflebottam: " When methane is present the flame of the safety-lamp flickers and a pale, non-luminous, slightly blue cap is seen above the ordinary flame." An expert miner, armed with the safety lamp properly trimmed for testing purpose, is thus able to tell at once if any considerable quantity of the gas is present. Fire-damp, unlike after-damp, is not poisonous, though like black damp being devoid of oxygen it will not support life. It does not poison but suffocates.

After-damp is the old name given to the mixture of gases caused by the explosion of fire-damp. Its deadly component is carbon monoxide which is extraordinarily poisonous. A percentage of even 0·4 of carbon monoxide will have a fatal result unless the person attacked is able to get into pure air quickly. After a fire-damp explosion the percentage may be anything from 1·0 to 5·0 per cent. Anyone caught in such an atmosphere would die in a few minutes.

Carbon monoxide is caused by the imperfect oxidation of carbon. Its generation can occasionally be seen in the hearth fire, the gas burning with a bluish lambent flame. It follows, as we have seen, upon an explosion of fire-damp thus:

$$2CH_4 + 7O = 4H_2O + CO_2 + CO$$

when CH_4=fire-damp and CO=carbon monoxide. It is also caused by what are termed gob fires.

We shall have occasion later to describe the gob, goaf, or waste, and it is sufficient here to note that

EARLY DAYS

in the process of mining the space formed by the extracting of the coal is filled in with rubbish which contains a certain amount of coal, slack, and dust. Occasionally fires start through spontaneous combustion in the waste, and owing to imperfect oxidation a considerable amount of carbon monoxide is generated. With proper oxidation carbon dioxide would be formed and the heavy, suffocating, but not actively poisonous black damp[1] would be obtained.

The gob fire is also the cause of the sulphuretted hydrogen which, under the name of white damp, choke damp, or gob-stink, has troubled the miner for centuries. It is poisonous and causes irritation to eyes, throat, and lungs.

We have digressed from the theme of our narrative in order shortly to describe the various kinds of 'damps' which threaten the health and life of the miner, because many people appear to imagine that the invention of the safety lamp by Sir Humphry Davy in 1815 solved the problem of explosions in mines. This is a complete inversion of the truth. In fact explosions still occur and the danger is still present, as may be seen from the terrible disasters at Courrières (France) and at Senghenydd (South Wales) in 1906 and 1913, disasters due to explosions which resulted in the loss of 1100 and 427 lives respectively. In the years

---

[1] Black damp is a mixture of nitrogen and carbon dioxide; air is a mixture of nitrogen and oxygen; after-damp is a mixture of nitrogen, carbon dioxide, and carbon monoxide.

following upon the invention of the safety lamps more explosions occurred than in the years preceding, for a very similar reason to that which results in more swimmers than non-swimmers losing their lives by drowning—a feeling of security causing risks to be taken which would not otherwise be even thought of.

In so far as the problem created by the presence of noxious gases has been solved, it has been solved mainly by improved ventilation.

It will readily be realized that in a pit of any depth, quite apart from explosion or poisonous gases, it is necessary to have some ventilation to render the air at all pure and the temperature tolerable. Sir John Cadman calculates that on the average the temperature rises 1° F. per every 72 ft. (12 fathoms) of depth. Under modern conditions of working, therefore, it is essential to have good ventilation in deep mines in consequence of the heat, but in the early days of the industry this consideration was hardly present as fifty fathoms was about the limit of working.

The earliest form of ventilation, apart from free ventilation obtained by adits similar to those used for drainage purposes and only possible in outcrop workings, was the furnace. This was developed in the first instance in Belgium where a surface furnace, drawing a current of air through the mine by means of air shafts and a chimney, was set up at the Liège mines some time before 1665. The surface furnace was not much used in

EARLY DAYS

England, its place being taken by a furnace placed at the bottom of the up-cast shaft. This created a current of air in the shaft which, in turn, drew fresh air down the down-cast shaft and caused the underground workings to be ventilated. This simple method continued to be the only one used until well into the nineteenth century, such small improvements as were made being in connection with the better direction of the air currents so set up. Air-doors, screens, and walls were being thought of in the mid-seventeenth century, but in the main ventilation was rudimentary and the conditions of working must have been entirely bad until the middle of the nineteenth century.

We thus see that in its early days the technical side of the industry was slowly progressing, but that even after seven centuries of experience it was not marked by any high technical achievement. The mines were still comparatively shallow, drainage had improved, but the dangers arising from noxious gases were only inadequately dealt with. The invention of the safety lamp had not reduced explosions but had rendered working possible in seams which could not perhaps otherwise have been worked, but at the same time had added to the miner's miseries by reducing the quantity of the light by which he worked—the Davy lamp only giving about one-fifth of a candle power—thus causing one of the most troublesome of miners' diseases—nystagmus.

We now propose shortly to describe the type of

men that worked under these conditions. It will be apparent from what follows how enormously these conditions of labour have changed and how greatly they have improved. Many causes have contributed to this change and amongst these causes are to be placed the improvement in general education affecting both owners, management and men, increased appreciation of employers of the rights of labour, and combination on the part of the men to see that their rights are observed.

At first the miner was a serf, and in Wales it is not improbable that he was also generally a criminal, there being some evidence to show that the Welsh regarded the sending of men to work in the mines as a suitable form of punishment for criminality.

The serf was, of course, bound for life to his lord to work on such terms as his lord thought fit. He did what he was told. He could be sold or given away. As against his lord he had no rights though the criminal law protected him from cruelty in the same way and almost to the same extent as the horse and dog are protected to-day. It is not probable that as a general rule the miner remained a serf in England after the middle of the fifteenth century, but in Scotland the colliers continued in a state of bondage until 1799, although an act had been passed in 1775 providing that, *except as regards persons then employed in the industry*, colliers should thereafter be treated as free labourers.

It must not, however, be imagined that this Act was the outcome of humanitarian sentiments, for as the preamble states "there are not a sufficient number of colliers ... in Scotland for working the quantity of coal ... necessarily wanted, and many new-discovered coals remain unwrought," and consequently it was decided that recruits must be attached to the industry by giving to all such the rights of free labourers.

These rights were small enough. So little indeed did the colliers appreciate the change that they considered themselves the victims of a trick on the part of their owners who, they thought, were simply attempting to get rid of the harigild money—a payment made to the serf when the serf's wife bore him a child and so increased the lord's property by, in effect, increasing his livestock.

With the abolition of life bondage it became necessary to substitute a shorter binding period. To-day the Scotch miner has gone to the very opposite extreme and customarily works on a day-to-day contract, whereas in England and Wales the fortnightly or weekly contract is usual. In times before the middle of the nineteenth century it was otherwise. The men, except those employed by butties, were usually bound for a year on terms fixed at the beginning of the binding period, generally August, as in the case of the agricultural labourer.

This yearly binding was the cause of a strike of

some magnitude which took place in Durham in 1765. The men complained that although they had bound themselves for a year beginning in August "the honourable gentlemen in the coal trade will not let us be free till the 11th of November of the ensuing year, . . . so the said pitmen are resolved not to work for or serve the said gentlemen in any of the collieries." The strike lasted for several weeks and, in the course of the disturbances resulting, the miners set fire to one of the Pelton Colliery pits.

It is of interest to note that throughout the above dispute the men at Hartley Colliery, having been well treated by the owner, Thomas Delavel, remained at work in appreciation of his kindness. It should be added that at that time in virtue of an Act passed in 1736 it was capital felony to set fire to a mine.

Even after the passing of the Factory Acts had protected to some slight extent the operatives in factories, the coal miner, the least of labourers it would seem in the estimation of the Legislature in those days, remained in the same desperate circumstances as had characterized his life in preceding centuries. Under-paid, degraded, heathen, they were of the lowly the lowest. In the words of Lord Bolingbroke : " These unhappy wretches scarce ever see the light of the sun ; they are buried in the bowels of the earth, where they work at a severe and dismal task, without the least prospect of being delivered from it. They subsist upon the coarsest and worst of fare. They have their health miserably impaired, and their lives cut short by being perpetually confined in the close vapours of these malignant minerals." In the same strain and writing in the same century (the eighteenth), Southey could say, speaking of Whitfield's missionary work among the colliers: "It was a matter of duty and sound policy that these people should not be left in a state of bestial ignorance—heathens, or worse than heathens—in the midst of a Christian country, and brutal as savages." We are reminded how the eloquence of Wesley wrought so on the rough minds of these hard men that their tears made white gutters run down their black cheeks.

Those were the days when women and children worked in collieries. Women and young children will never again work underground. It is within the recollection of the writer how, during the war, when lack of labour was keenly felt and the output of the much-needed coal was dropping and dropping, a certain ardent lady wrote to say that she would collect and lead a large body of women volunteer workers to labour in the mines. The offer was magnificent and the women would doubtless have acquitted themselves well in this as in so many other hard and difficult tasks, but it was impossible even to consider such an offer, for both owners and miners were utterly opposed to woman labour in the mines.

The first great step in what was to prove a

long series of legislative enactments designed to improve the conditions of labour in collieries was taken in 1842 when Lord Ashley's Bill passed both Houses and became law. This Bill, designed to abolish the employment underground of women and young children, was the outcome of the report of the Commissioners for enquiring into the Condition of Children Employed in Mines, a report based on a lengthy and close enquiry into the condition of mine labour and one which expresses in a clear and graphic manner the appalling conditions existing in the fourth year of the reign of Queen Victoria.

Those were the days when hewers made 3s. 9d. a day for twelve hours' work, when putters, i.e. the men who loaded the tubs, trolleys or trams, received 2s. 6d. a day, and when under-ground horse-keepers received 14s. a week. These were the Northumberland figures and were rather higher than the average for the country. Thus in Lancashire and Cheshire a collier (or hewer) earned from 14s. to 16s. a week; the drawer anything from 1s. 9d. to 9s.

The hours of labour were rarely less than 10 hours a day and in some districts were considerably in excess of that. Usually the children had to endure the longest hours. Thus, in the Oldham district, we read that "when in full employment the adult coal-getters work 9, 10 and 11 hours a day; and the children and young persons employed in bringing to the pit bottom the coal which they have hewn, about 2 hours longer, or 11, 12 and 13 hours, which are sometimes protracted to 14 and 15." In Derbyshire "from 13 to 16 hours are reckoned a day's work . . . 8 hours make half a day's work."

In some districts children and women were reckoned in terms of parts of a man. Thus when a boy went to work at seven or eight years of age he was considered to be equal to one-eighth part of a man and got 5s. a month. At ten years of age he was deemed the equivalent of two-eighths of a man; at thirteen years, three-eighths; at fifteen years, one-half; at eighteen years, three-fourths; at twenty-one the whole of a man. A girl at sixteen was regarded as the equivalent of one half of a man, and at that equivalent remained whatever her age might be.

The sort of life which was lived by these children, described by one of the witnesses as "worse than the slavery of the West Indies," may be judged from the evidence of Mrs. Roker, the mother of Thomas Roker, a pit-boy. This woman informed the sub-Commissioners that her son "was aged about six years and seven months, and that he had been down the pit about a month or six weeks. The boy was at school at three years old, and his father wished to make him a better scholar before he went down. Always puts him to bed early, because he must get up every working morning at three o'clock; and he often rubs his eyes when he is woke, and says he has only just been to sleep.

He gets up at 3 a.m., and goes down the pit at 4 a.m. He gets his dinner directly he comes home, about 4.30 p.m., or 4.45 p.m., and then he washes himself and goes to bed between six and seven; so that he will never be up more than two hours from the pit for eating, washing and playing. When his son gets a little more hardened to the pit, his father means to send him to night-school, and stop one hour off his sleep."

Thomas Roker's was neither an unusual nor an excessively bad case. There are instances quoted of children of three and four working in the mines and one of the Sub-Commissioners states that "some are so young they go in their bed-gowns." The statistical returns show, indeed, that a considerable proportion of the employees were children under thirteen and, though it was rare for a child of less than six years to be employed, they often commenced work between the age of seven and eight, and usually between the age of eight and nine.

The statistics showing the proportion of adults, females and children are as follows :—

District	Adults M.	F.	13 to 18 M.	F.	Under 13 M.	F.
England ..	1	·018	·277	·019	·226	·011
Scotland ..	1	·211	·275	·155	·143	·070
Wales ..	1	·147	·302	·046	·169	·010

from which it will be seen that in England there were half as many children as adults employed in the mines, while in Scotland there were almost as many women and children employed as adult males, the proportion being ·854 and 1 respectively. It is therefore fair to lay some stress on the conditions under which these poor children and women toiled.

The responsibility for child labour must not be assigned entirely to the colliery proprietors of those days. There is much evidence to show that in a great number of districts the Durham and Northumberland practice, whereby the owner bound his employees for a year, was replaced by the 'butty' system. Under this system[1] the owner of the colliery agreed with a contractor to pay so much a ton for coal delivered at the shaft bottom and left the contractor or 'butty' to arrange how he would for the hewing and transporting of the coal at and from the coal-face to the shaft. The 'butty' employed the hewers and trammers, etc., and paid them sometimes in kind, often at a public-house owned by the 'butty.'

There is some evidence to show that in many cases the owners were opposed to women labour (which only existed in England so far as underground labour was concerned in Yorkshire and Lancashire) and did not favour the employment

---

[1] The system still exists in a modified form, but, of course, all the abuses touched upon in the following pages have long disappeared.

of very young children, but it would seem that the low rates of wages compelled the parents in many instances practically to drive their children into the mines to earn by their toil some 3s. or 5s. a week. In Scotland also the mothers who were mainly employed in the roads dragging the tubs on hands and knees along low roads took their children with them to help them in their drudgery by pushing the tubs from behind.

The conditions under which these poor folk worked in those days were bad. It is hoped that what follows is not a gross exaggeration for it is based on a careful perusal of the Report of the Commissioners above referred to. It must be remembered, however, that the Commissioners had in mind a great evil and their report is consequently coloured; the following description is not, however, based solely upon that report but upon other sources, particularly the evidence given before the Committee which enquired in 1835 into the causes of accidents at mines and upon the Midland Mining Commission Report.

Men were employed mainly at the coal-face in hewing and putting, i.e. cutting the coal from the seam and loading it into the tubs. Women were mainly employed in Scotland, Lancashire and Yorkshire in pulling the tubs from the coal-face to the shaft and in winding coal by hand winches and in stages up to the surface. Children were mainly employed in opening and closing the air gates in order to allow the tubs to pass through and in hauling coal along the roads underground.

With the above preamble we will attempt a description of life in a mine in 1842.

The men at the coal-face worked sometimes standing, sometimes sitting and sometimes lying down according to the nature of the seam and the type of holing adopted. Usually they were entirely naked. The women, pulling or pushing the tubs, would crawl along the roadways which in many cases were only thirty inches high and sometimes less. They brought the tubs to where the men were working naked and the putter would then fill the tub, and the woman—who usually wore trousers and a shirt and nothing else—would then drag the tub to the shaft by means of a chain round her waist and passing between her legs to the tub.

Where women were not employed this business of tub-dragging was done partly by ponies and partly by children. The ponies worked along the main haulage roads and the children along the low roadways leading from the main haulage roads to the coal-face. The height of these subsidiary roadways usually depended on the thickness of the coal seam and were sometimes not more than twenty inches high, so that the child dragging the heavy tub, which did not run on wheels but on iron slids, had to crawl along on hands and knees. The girls worked in trousers and shift, sometimes in their shift alone. Thus Mary Barnett aged fourteen : " I work always without stockings, or shoes, or trousers ; I wear nothing but my shift ; I have to go up to the headings (i.e. coal-face) with the men ; they are all naked there ; I am got well used to that, and don't care much about it ; I was afraid at first and did not like it."

These girls earned very small wages. A woman of twenty employed as a drawer would work for 2s. a day or less, whereas a man of that age would want 3s. 6d. They worked fearfully hard. Thus Ann Thomas, windlass woman of South Wales : " I find the work very hard ; two women always work the windlass below ground. We wind up 800 loads [a load was about $1\frac{1}{2}$ cwt.]. Men do not like the winding, it is too hard work for them."

Always the mines are dark, always they are and will be dirty, but to-day they are dry, the roads are well kept and reasonably high, and the air is fairly fresh and healthy. Then often the mines were wet and the ventilation was only directed so as to clear the face, the interior of the colliery being very insufficiently aerated. It was in the centre where the roadways were that the women and children mainly worked. Some of these children were found working ankle-deep in water or crawling through pools. Once a little girl of seven years of age, who was supposed to be watching an air gate upon the proper working of which the safety of all in the mine might have depended, was found asleep, her lamp having gone out and the rats having eaten her meal of bread and cheese.

We all remember Dickens' description of the apprenticing of Oliver Twist and how narrowly he escaped from the clutches of Gamfield the chimney sweep. That was "a nasty trade," as Mr. Limbkins the Poor Law guardian said, but it could hardly have been worse than the trade of butty's boy to which thousands of lads were condemned—we can hardly use any other word—in the early decades of last century.[1]

This practice of apprenticing was extremely common in South Staffordshire. In the words of the Midland Mining Commissioner: "These apprentices are paupers or orphans, and are wholly in the power of the butties; such is the demand of this class of children by the butties that there are scarcely any boys in the Union Workhouses of Walsall, Wolverhampton, Dudley and Stourbridge; these boys are sent on trial to the butties between the ages of eight and nine, and at nine are bound as apprentices for *twelve years*, that is, to the age of twenty-one years complete; notwithstanding this long apprenticeship, there is nothing whatever in the coal-mines to learn beyond a little dexterity, readily acquired by short practice, the orphan whom necessity has driven into a workhouse is made to labour in the mines until the age of twenty-one, solely for the benefit of another."

These apprentices received no pay at all. They

---

[1] Even greater abuses existed in some other trades in regard to apprenticing. It was a very widespread evil.

were kept in clothes and food and shelter by their masters and were put to the hardest and most dangerous tasks. The overseer at Oldham gave evidence before the Sub-Commissioner to the effect that causes of cruelty to apprentices in coal-mines were common and he himself had " to summon three cases within the last week, where boys had been unmercifully used." Thrashing and kicking were the common means of keeping these lads at their work, but sometimes, when a boy refused even under blows to work in a place where an explosion might occur or other specially dangerous risk be encountered, he was dragged before the magistrate who promptly committed the ' offender ' to prison.

The apprenticeship system was almost entirely restricted to the districts where the working of the coal was chartered out to butties, and it was these butties who were responsible for a great many of the evils under which those who worked in mines laboured.

The Midland Mining Commission, who in the person of Thomas Tancred reported on the social position of the mining population of South Staffordshire in 1843, made it clear that the colliery proprietors where the butty system was in operation had little or nothing to do with the conditions of work in the mine. The butty, charterer, or contractor 'took on the mine' at such and such a price, it might be £300 or £400. For that he was entitled to work the mine and receive for every ton of coal delivered at shaft bottom so much a ton. The butty being of the labouring classes and, like most labouring people of those days, uneducated, was without any financial resources except his savings which were rarely sufficient to allow of his putting down the capital required under the charter. As a consequence the colliery proprietor permitted him to pay the capital outlay by a system of deductions on the charter tonnage rates.

Some butties, besides paying the miners, found the candles, powder, timber (except in the main haulage roads), horses. They drove levels and did other dead work such as laying rails. In a case in which all these out-of-pockets were paid by the butties, the terms of the charter were as follows:—

CHARTER PRICE, £109 15s. 0d.

Coal	Charter price per ton
	s. d.
Best coal	2 8
Lumps	1 9
Rough slack ..	1 2
Fine slack ..	0 10½

It followed almost of necessity that the butties overworked, underpaid, and oppressed the men working for them. The colliery proprietors frequently had no knowledge of pit-working and had never been down a pit. They frequently relied entirely on the butty for the proper working of the pit and appointed no agents, viewers or managers to look after the underground working on their behalf. As the Commissioner said in contrasting the probabilities of employment under a charter and employment directly under a colliery proprietor: " To illustrate this by an example taken from one of the more generally known and familiar occupations of workmen, which, let one ask, would be likely to be the preferable system for the employment of labourers in husbandry—the common one of a respectable farmer hiring, managing and paying his own workmen, or a system of contracting with a man of the labouring class to grow him his corn, hay, turnips, beans, etc., and to perform all the labour on the farm at a charter of so much a ton on the produce raised, the farmer having nothing to do with his land but to see that it was not improperly exhausted, leaving the hiring and treating of the labourers to the discretion of the contractor ? " To ask the question was to answer it.

The wages generally and all over the country were in those days far below anything known to-day, but the following list of prices paid to holers and pikemen (i.e. hewers or colliers) in the Bilston area are instructive, especially when it is borne in mind that this is for a twelve-hour day and a man only averaged about two hundred days a year

EARLY DAYS

instead of being as to-day, if he so desired, in practically continuous employment.

Year	Day's Wage
	s. d. s. d.
1833	3 0 – 3 3
1834	3 6
1835	3 3 – 2 6
1836	3 6 – 3 9
1837	3 9
1838	3 9
1839	3 9
1840	3 9 – 3 6
1841	3 3 – 3 0
1842	2 9 – 2 6
1843	2 6

A wage of 3s. a day for two hundred days gives an income of £30 a year, and although meat was but 5d. a pound and cheese 7½d. a pound, and although the pitmen got two quarts of beer a day and their coals free, we can well believe the words of one of the witnesses when speaking of the miners' domestic economy, " they eat all they have at the beginning of the week and towards the end of the week they get things how they can by running into debt and clamming."

The solution was usually found by everybody in the family working, and when the family was large and healthy (a rare conjunction in those days) the miner was comfortably off and on a fair way to become in turn a butty.

But we grow tedious. Enough has been said to show that real evils, real grievances of wrong then existed. The people were patient. They toiled and suffered much and complained but little. The public conscience was awakening. The responsibilities, the heavy responsibilities, which fall upon the employers of labour were beginning to be realized, and Parliament commenced to take a hand in controlling the conditions of labour in mines.

The first great Act of Parliament designed to mitigate the conditions of the mining population was the direct outcome of the Commission which had enquired into the employment of children. That Commission's report was presented by Command to Parliament in April, 1842, and by the August of that year Lord Ashley's Bill " To prohibit the Employment of Women and Girls in Mines and Collieries, to regulate the Employment of Boys, and to make other Provisions relating to Persons working therein " had become law.

There was a certain amount of opposition to it on the part of the colliery owners. An honourable member of the House of Commons could be found to say in defence of the practice of binding apprentices to butties that the occupation of miner " was generally considered a remarkably pleasant and cheerful employment," and a noble Lord in the other House adventured the opinion that " the measure might be regarded as the commencement of a series of grievances which would

EARLY DAYS 31

be got up for the purpose of working on that hypocritical humanity which feigned so much." Humanity, hypocritical and otherwise, does not appear to have been strongly implanted in the heart of that particular Peer, for he also expressed the view that " some seams of coal *require* the employment of women "—referring, of course, to those thin seams in which the roadways as then cut were so low that only a woman or a child could crawl through them with any expedition.

Under this Act, as finally passed, the employment of women and female children in mines underground was, as from a date fixed, made illegal. No male child under ten years of age was to be permitted to work at a mine. Apprenticeship of girls was avoided as from a date fixed, and no boy could henceforward be apprenticed under ten years of age or for an apprenticeship exceeding eight years except in cases of skilled colliery trades such as that of engine-wright. Existing apprenticeship deeds were modified accordingly. A Mines Inspector was appointed for the purpose of seeing that the provisions of the Act were complied with and in order to report on the social condition of the mining population. He was in no way to concern himself with the management of mines, and in fact the first Mines Inspector, Mr. Tremenheere, had been a School Inspector and knew nothing of the technical side of mine management.

Several minor provisions, such as those forbidding the payment of wages at public-houses, the placing of children under fifteen in charge of winding engines, and making liable the agent or butty for the penalties imposed upon the owner where it was proved that the illegality had been committed by the agent or butty without the privity of the owner, are contained in this great emancipating Act; but the main thing effected by it was the abolition of female and infant labour from the mines underground.

The next great steps in the history of the industry were connected with the Inspection of Mines ushered in by the Act of 1850, and the regulation of the industry commenced by the Act of 1855. Of these we shall speak in the next chapter where we shall shortly describe the history of the industry from 1843 to the present day.

CHAPTER II

LATER LEGISLATION

THE constant recurrence of colliery explosions brought somewhat frequently before the attention of the public the question of the conditions of the coal-mining industry in the forties and fifties of last century. The disclosures made by the Commissioners who had enquired into the employment of women and children had convinced many thinking men that all was not well, and as explosion followed explosion it was felt that something more remained to be done than had been accomplished by Lord Ashley's Act.

That act, as we have seen, dealt only with the conditions of certain types of labour. The inspector appointed under it was only concerned with the social conditions of the workers. He had nothing to do with the technical management of the mines. It was beginning to be apparent, however, that the technical management left almost as much to be desired as did the labour conditions of the industry.

We remind the reader that in those days no special qualification was required in order for a person to be placed in control of mine management. In many cases, as we have seen, the entire business of underground management was in the charge of butties or chartermen, who, in the majority of cases, were quite ignorant and in some cases absolutely illiterate. The colliery owners in some districts had very little more knowledge of what was going on in their mines than have the royalties owners to-day. The Government had no means of judging how matters stood, for no Government Inspectors (apart from what we may term the social investigator, Mr. Tremenheere) had been appointed. No learned Society considered it as part of its duty to enquire into or consider the problem of this important and advancing industry. No School of Mines existed. Apart from the Sunderland Association created in 1813 (largely in consequence of a disaster at Felling Colliery) to enquire into the cause of colliery explosions no society existed for the specific object of improving the technical side of the industry. Such was the condition of affairs when in 1854 the Government appointed two Commissioners—Sir Henry de la Beche and Dr. Lyon Playfair—to enquire into the various 'damps,' their generation and means to be taken to avoid disasters arising therefrom.

The report of these two Commissioners showed a great disparity between the conditions in different districts. Differences due partly to variations in the natural conditions but mainly to the fact that some collieries were managed with skill and knowledge whereas others were carried on so ignorantly and

LATER LEGISLATION   35

badly that it was a matter for surprise how they could have been worked in such a state.

In the following year an explosion occurred at Oldbury among other places, and Sir Henry de la Beche was sent to investigate. He discovered that no system of ventilation existed at all. In other cases investigated it was found that owing to laxity on the part of the management and ignorance or foolhardiness on the part of the workers, risks out of all proportion to those necessary under proper management were daily being run. The case for Government inspection was becoming unanswerable. It is true that in the event of a fatal accident arising the coroner for the district was supposed to institute an enquiry, but it was by no means clear that such an enquiry took place in every case. The coroners' records were found to be very defective and no eagerness on the part of the owners to court enquiries of such a nature was apparent. But quite apart from the completeness or adequacy of coroners' inquests something more was wanted beside the somewhat unsatisfactory expedient of trying to mop up spilt milk. It was desired to prevent disasters instead of merely explaining them, and it was felt that the best way of doing this was to have a Government inspection which it was believed could hardly fail to achieve two purposes : make colliery proprietors see that their mines were properly managed and place the Government in possession of the facts relating to mines improperly managed. It was indeed proposed by a coroner's jury, after the Ardsley disaster, that the Government should go further and actually regulate by Act of Parliament the manner in which mines should be conducted. That reform, however, as yet lay in the future. The immediate aim of the Government was to secure inspection, and this aim was achieved by the Act of 1850 " For Inspection of Coal Mines in Great Britain " which was amplified by the Act of 1855 which also contained clauses in the nature of regulations for the management of coal mines.

The Act of 1850, in addition to compelling owners to produce mine maps and plans to the inspector on demand, to give notice of accidents, and imposing penalties for obstructing inspectors (a clause inserted because of Lord Londonderry's assertion that if an inspector came to his mines he would not allow him to go down, and if he did go down he could stay there), had as its main provision the following clause :

" That it shall be lawful for any such Inspector as aforesaid to enter, inspect, and examine any Coal-Mine or Colliery, and the Works and Machinery belonging thereto, at all reasonable Times and Seasons, by Day or Night, but so as not to impede or obstruct the workings of the said Coal-Mine or Colliery, and to make Inquiry into and touching the State and Condition of such Coal-Mine or Colliery, Works and Machinery, and the Ventilation of such Coal-Mine or Colliery, and the Mode of

LATER LEGISLATION

Lighting or using Lights in the same, and into all Matters and Things connected with or relating to the Safety of the Persons employed in or about the same."

In the words of R. N. Boyd :[1] " The Act of 1850 did little else than establish the principle of underground inspection. The innovation was received with more or less dissatisfaction by the colliery proprietors. They objected to a system which authorized a Government Official to pry into the management of their works, and dreaded the possibility of an interference in their trade. Some ... feared that the Government inspectors would be scientific men who might recommend alterations impossible to carry out or ruinously expensive." In fact neither the colliery owners' fears nor the Government's hopes were justified. Only four inspectors were appointed and they were expressly informed that it was no part of their duty to enforce any particular mode of ventilation or working. As a result of the fewness of the inspectors and the limitation of their powers their appointment had practically no effect one way or another upon the industry. There were some 1200 collieries in the country at that time, and even had the inspectors been the most energetic of men, they could hardly have inspected all the collieries under two or three years. Colliery proprietors consequently began to forget that inspectors existed, magistrates did not lean in

[1] *Coal Mines Inspection*, p. 105,

favour of prosecutions under the Act, and the inspectors' powers were too small to enable them to enforce or effect anything relative to management or working.

Meanwhile disasters continued frequently to occur. In 1851 no fewer than 1062 persons were killed by accidents in collieries. In that year explosions, involving in each case the loss of more than thirty lives, occurred at Nitshill Colliery, Workington and Rawmarsh. In one of the many other cases where minor explosions occurred it was found that no system of ventilation existed, and in another case that the disaster had been caused by an air-door—the proper opening and closing of which is always a matter of vital importance—being kept propped open. In some collieries it was found that the air-ways had become blocked by falls and were useless, in others that the bad gases were got rid of by the rudimentary and dangerous practice of burning them out, in yet others that there was no separate down-cast and up-cast shaft. It was apparent that conditions left much to be desired, and in 1855 the Government found it necessary to strengthen the powers of the inspectors and also to lay down certain rules for the regulation of all coal-mines. These rules, which marked the commencement of Coal Mine Regulation, were as follows:

" 1. An adequate amount of Ventilation shall be constantly produced at all Collieries to dilute and render harmless noxious Gases to such an extent

LATER LEGISLATION

as that the Working Places of the Pits and Levels of such Collieries shall under ordinary circumstances be in a fit state for working:

2. Every Shaft or Pit which is out of use, or used only as an Air-Pit, shall be securely fenced:

3. Every Working and Pumping Pit or Shaft shall be properly fenced when not at work:

4. Every Working and Pumping Pit or Shaft where the natural Strata under ordinary circumstances are not safe shall be securely cased or lined:

5. Every Working Pit or Shaft shall be provided with some proper means of signalling from the Bottom of the Shaft to the Surface, and from the Surface to the Bottom of the Shaft:

6. A proper Indicator to show the Position of the Load in the Pit or Shaft, and also an adequate Brake shall be attached to every Machine worked by Steam or Water Power used for lowering or raising Persons:

7. Every Steam Boiler shall be provided with a proper Steam Gauge, Water Gauge, and Safety Valve.'"

In addition the owners were empowered to make rules, to be approved by the Secretary of State, for the management and working of their mines, and the inspectors were authorized to see that the rules so made were carried out.

These rules were, it will be observed, extremely simple and were drafted in the most general terms.

The need of them showed that the industry had not yet reached universally a high state of technical achievement. Signs were not wanting, however, to show that the industry, quite apart from interference on the part of the legislature, was beginning to take itself more seriously and was by internal action endeavouring to attain a position amongst the industries of the country worthy of its importance. A School of Mines was established in 1851, and an agitation began having for its object the spread of technical education amongst those who had charge of the safety of the men and the management of the mines. In 1852 the Institute of Mining Engineers of the North of England was formed for the purpose of promoting the theory, art and practice of mining. Throughout the fifties learned societies which had hitherto paid little attention to the problems connected with mining were beginning to study the many great and important problems which form a scientific point of view the coal industry had and still has to offer.

Much, however, yet remained to be done. In South Wales one of H.M. Inspectors could report that he had " little expectation of being able to prevent, without other assistance of a penal kind, the effects of that cold-blooded apathy which disregards the lives and limbs of human beings "— this, it is true, was before the Act of 1855 had been passed, but the position was not substantially improved by the passing of that measure.

It became indeed more and more clear as Act

succeeded Act and explosion, explosion that something more than paper rules were required to cleanse the industry of the many blots and stains that still attached to it, and the hope for the future lay rather in the fact that the colliery owners were beginning to awake to a realization of their responsibilities than in Parliamentary interference. It is of significance that the Act of 1855, extending the provisions of the Act of 1850, which the owners had half-heartedly opposed, was largely due to the action of the owners and to the movement set on foot by the Coal Trade Association of Northumberland and Durham.

It must not be imagined that during these years when the coal mining industry was awakening from its state of lethargy that the miners had remained dumb. The Miners' Federation of Great Britain and Ireland, founded at Wakefield in 1841, had quickly grown into a powerful organization with a membership of one hundred thousand. Under the able leadership of Martin Jude and aided by the skill of W. P. Roberts (who received a retainer of £1000 a year to act as legal adviser) it had frequently been able, despite the repressive legislation of those days, to assert itself and attain some of its many desires.

Broadly speaking the miners aimed at better wages, shorter hours, better education, more inspection and the giving of power to the inspectors to interfere with the management. The first two aims were the cause of many strikes, mostly unsuccessful, the remaining aims were chiefly fought for with the political weapon, and the action of the Miners' Federation was undoubtedly a contributing cause to the passing of the Acts of 1850, 1855 and 1860. They completely failed, however, in their attempts to give to the inspectors the power of management as distinct from inspection. The Government was firm in its opinion that the proper course to pursue in the interest of the industry was to place upon the owners the duty of managing their collieries safely and efficiently and to impose upon the owners the responsibility of carrying out such duty properly.

The Act of 1860 above referred to was in effect a re-enactment of the Act of 1855 with certain extensions of the power of the inspectors and certain additions to the statutory regulations already in existence. It also made an important amendment to the Act of 1842 relating to the age at which boys should commence work in a mine. The minimum age which had hitherto been ten was altered to twelve, and it was further provided that in future the winding engine should not be in charge of any person except a male of eighteen years or upward. By an amending Act of 1862 it was further provided that " it shall not be lawful for the Owner of an existing Mine to employ any Person in working within such Mine, or to permit any Person to be in such Mine for the purpose of working therein, unless there are in communication with every Seam of such Mine for the time

LATER LEGISLATION

being at work at least Two Shafts or Outlets, separated by natural Strata of not less than Ten Feet in breadth, by which Shafts and Outlets distinct Means of Ingress and Egress are available to the Persons employed in the Mine."

The need for this provision requires some explanation. Already in 1813 Buddle, one of the pioneers of the Coal Industry, had pointed out the dangers and drawbacks flowing from the common practice of obtaining an up-cast and down-cast shaft by sinking one shaft and dividing it into two parts by a brattice or partition—usually of wood. In 1835 the practice had again been condemned by several witnesses before the Commission which sat to consider the cause of explosions in mines. The danger was obvious. It was only necessary for the partition to be destroyed and the whole system of ventilation broke down. An explosion of any strength was almost certain to destroy and damage the brattice and cause the death by suffocation of all underground. No legislative action was taken, however, and the practice of single divided shafts continued at many collieries.

The country was awakened, however, to the evil of this cheap but dangerous practice by the Hartley disaster which occurred on the 16th January, 1862. The actual event did not follow the predictions of those who had foreseen the dangers arising from the partitioned single shaft. They had expected disaster through the partition being destroyed from below whereas at Hartley it was destroyed from above by the beam of the pumping engine breaking and falling down the shaft, breaking the partition, loosening the walls of the shaft and entombing 204 men in what was now an absolutely unventilated pit.

At once all was energy and action. Shaft sinkers and miners worked at the utmost pressure and in face of the greatest danger to dig out the entombed men. Their heroic combats with choke-damp, water and falling debris at length enabled them to fight their way through to where the men had been working, but it was to discover not men but corpses. Not one had survived.

The year following (1863) was very noticeable for the activity of the men's unions. For a moment the question of safety was allowed to recede into the background, though one of the aims of the men's leaders was the tightening up of the rules relating to safety. The main aims, however, were better education, a higher age limit, a reduction of hours of labour in the case of youths, and payment by weight only.

The question of payment by weight had long been a bone of contention between the owners and the men. Prior to the Act of 1860 the practice had been to reckon the tub or corve as holding so much and to pay in effect so much a tub, etc. for coal got. The men complained that they were cheated and that the weight they were credited with was substantially less than the true weight. In one district it was alleged that a tub which when made held five hundredweight was found to increase in size as it grew older and had to be repaired, with the result that it eventually held seven hundredweight though the man filling it was only credited with five.

It was believed that the Act of 1860 had met this objection by providing that the men should be entitled to appoint at their own cost a person (called a checkweigher) to check the weighing, measuring or gauging of the coal got with a view to seeing that the men he was appointed by were not credited with too low an output. The men, however, still contended that their interests were not sufficiently protected and that payment ought to be by weight only as, granted the use of proper weights, there could be no possibility, such as existed where the coal was measured or gauged, of the calculated total of the output being computed too low.

On this point the men were of course looking solely to their own interests and were pressing an obviously fair claim. On the other points they were largely in the region of idealism and had consequently great difficulty in making good their demands. Hardly more than twenty years had passed since Lord Ashley's Act had abolished the employment of infants; as yet the principle of universal education was by no means established; until now neither the owners, Parliament nor the State had realized that efficiency depends upon technical knowledge extending far beyond rule-ofthumb methods. As a consequence the men's leaders' demands for improved education of boys and the need for the certification of managers were opposed by both the owners and by many of the men ; the lifting of the age limit from ten to twelve was regarded, both by the parents of the children affected and by their employers, as economically unsound and as tending to laziness and generally as idealistic, unnecessary and unwise. For the moment nothing was done and it was not until the people generally had seen the great value and gain arising from education, and until, as part of that great movement, the owners had begun to realize that their interests would be safer in the hands of a man who combined theoretical knowledge with practical experience than in those of one who possessed experience, possibly of bad conditions, only, that it became possible to place on the Statute Book the Acts of 1870 and 1872, the one of a general nature affecting, and affecting vitally, every industry in this country, the latter relating to the coal-mining industry alone.

Of one of these Acts, the " Act to provide for public Elementary Education in England and Wales," we do not propose to speak, for that Act affected the coal industry to no greater degree than every other trade or occupation. Of the second of these Acts, that of 1872, " To Consolidate and Amend the Acts relating to the Regulation of Coal-Mines and certain other Mines," we must at least touch upon, for it was this Act more than any other legislative enactment which ushered in the present era of high attainment and technical excellence which so sharply divides the coal industry of to-day from what it was when women and children were being driven by chartermasters in the early decades of last century.

In general and apart from one vital part the 1872 Act merely codified, strengthened and improved the Acts which had gone before. The minimum age, except in certain circumstances, was fixed at twelve and special provision was made to enable children employed to attain the necessary standard of education. The clause in the 1860 Act relating to checkweighing was modified, and the men's claim that payment should be by weight, and not by measuring or gauging, was conceded. The earlier statutory regulations were considerably amplified and the duties on the part of the owners and the powers of the inspectors relative to mines inspection extended. Breaches of the Truck Acts were rendered more difficult and made the subject of penal clauses. All these, however, were merely an extension of principles already conceded, principles which had been of little avail in improving either the safety or the efficiency of the industry, but in addition there was a new departure destined vitally to affect and improve the industry. The principle of certification was conceded, and in future, except in the case of mines employing less than thirty persons below ground, no mine could be managed by a person unless he had received a certificate of competency, which certificate could only be given to those who had succeeded in passing an examination to be regulated in the manner provided by the Act.

The enactment of this part of the Act of 1872 marked in our opinion a turning-point in the history of the industry. Several modifying Acts followed, the most important of which are the Coal Mines Regulation Acts of 1887 and 1911, but none contained any such momentous provision as this provision which so enormously improved the technical side of the industry that it is difficult to believe that only seventy years lie between our present day and those times which the Commissioners who were sitting in 1849 describe. Before the Act of 1872 passed many collieries were ably managed and efficiently run, already a colliery had created a record by winding one thousand tons of coal in a single shift, but such cases, and there were many such, of good management depended entirely on the existence of special individual ability. The Legislature, the State, the People, the Government, all those somewhat nebulous and powerful entities that are supposed to look after the welfare of the country, had hitherto been content to allow a vital and dangerous industry, employing a considerable proportion of the working population, to be managed by men who might be competent and who might be absolutely ignorant and incompetent. In future, though there might be the widest difference in the personal ability of managers, there was a standard set up to which all had to attain. Mine management instead of being a mere trade had become a profession.

The result was that the whole tone of the industry was lifted and, as year succeeds year, the upward movement thus commenced continues, so that to-day the British coal-mining industry is second to none in the world in achievement, and a body of men has been raised and trained who will be able to carry on whatever the future may have in store in the way of difficulties—and they are not likely to be few.

With the passing of the 1872 Act we consider that the present era commences. We do not propose to review the later legislation. The Acts of 1887 and 1911 are merely extensions of the Act of 1872. The so-called Eight Hours Act of 1908 and the Minimum Wages Act of 1912 we shall have occasion to mention when we come to consider the questions of hours and wages. We thus conclude our short account of the history of the industry and pass in the succeeding chapters to consider present conditions, and problems, and future difficulties.

CHAPTER III

THE WORKING OF A MODERN COLLIERY

WE hold strongly the view that the colliery owners of this country have to-day a legitimate grievance. They have conducted a great industry with marked ability and success. They, unlike many other captains of industry, have not profiteered during the war. They have in very numerous instances built for their workpeople admirable houses. The safety standard of British mines is the highest in the world. Yet to-day they have had to stand by patiently while bitter things have been said about them. The very nature of the controversy which has raged around nationalization has inevitably caused a great many hard things to be said about private ownership. Many of these complaints and criticisms, though true, press, in our view, most unfairly upon private owners and particularly on the managers of mines who, like the miners, are the paid employees of the owners and whose business it is to see that the mines are conducted as efficiently, as economically, as safely and as humanely as possible. These complaints and criticisms press unfairly, not because they are unfair, but because they arise out of a state of affairs which has come down to us from past ages when very different ideals and aims were sought after. They are unfair because these complaints and criticisms are not special to the coal industry but could be made and hurled against any other industry in any other country to-day.

We must not be understood to suggest that proper complaints and just criticism should not be made, but we warn the public not to assume that the coal owner is worse than his peer in other industries or in other countries, for we say with some confidence and some knowledge that he is a worthy representative of the business class which has done so much to make this country what it is— the most prosperous trading community in the world with the possible exception of America whose natural resources are altogether superior to our own.

We hope indeed that one of the results of this book will be to weaken the *argumentum ad hominem* as employed by the protagonists in the struggle which we have little doubt will rage before any fundamental change is made in the method of conducting the industry. It is idle for either side to attempt to strengthen their case by vilifying or traducing their opponents, for the truth is that both the coal owners and the coal miners are very good fellows.

This might be thought to be mere sycophantism were it not susceptible of proof. The proof may be made by a general and a particular argument. The general reason is that as the coal industry employs a tenth of the entire working population its members can hardly be a lazy, indolent and selfish body of men unless we are prepared to concede that those attributes are the mark of our victorious and successful people. The particular reason is to be found as regards the owners in two facts and as regards the men in two facts, viz.: (1) The owners voluntarily surrendered all but 5 per cent of their excess profits, for it must be remembered that, as a result of the Coal Mines Control Agreement in conjunction with the E.P.D. Act, the profits received by the mine owners are subject to the 80 per cent Excess Profit Duty and the 15 per cent Coal Mines Excess Payment, the combined effort of which is that the retainable profits can never exceed 5 per cent above the profits standard prescribed for each colliery by the Finance (No. 2) Act, 1915, which is the average of any two out of the three trading years immediately preceding the war, or, in certain cases, of any four out of the six of such years. (2) Of all the employers in the country the colliery owners made the best provision for the re-employment of their former workpeople who had enlisted into His Majesty's Forces. As a result, although some three hundred thousand miners were demobilized by March of 1919 (a rate far greater than that attained for any other type of worker), hardly any demobilized miner had to receive the unemployment dole. We were actively connected with the organization of the machinery which achieved this result and we are therefore in a position to state authoritatively that it could never have been accomplished had it not been that the colliery proprietors of this country did everything in their power to reinstate ex-soldiers, though in many cases this meant carrying on their business for a time at a lower profit than would otherwise have been the case and under great difficulties owing to the shortage of working places.

The men, on the other hand, have proved their right to be regarded as at least equal in patriotism and worth to the average of the people of this country by the fact that out of a total of about 1,000,000, 400,000 enlisted, and of this total 300,000 enlisted voluntarily. As a body they fought extremely well and bravely. They formed the majority of the Guards, they took a prominent part in the breaking of the Hindenburg line and in the victory at Messines. The men that remained conceded the principle of dilution, in many instances abandoned such customary holidays as those involved in the five-day week, and worked their best and their hardest to keep production up. There was, and is, a regrettable amount of absenteeism, but, generally speaking, those best qualified to judge think that the miners, both those who enlisted and those who remained, did well, and throughout the war were wisely and patriotically led.

We feel that the above should be stated and that this is the place to state it. We have seen what the condition of the industry was at the close of the Napoleonic wars; we have described the conditions under which men, and women, and little children laboured then. We will now describe a modern mine. The difference is so great that we have felt to be due the above Confession of Faith—faith in the owners and in the men.

A really up-to-date colliery usually consists of three parts: The mine, the screens, the washery.[1] We will therefore conduct the reader into the mine, to the working face, thence to the screens and finally to where the washed coal falls from the washery shoots into the waiting railway trucks below. He will find that a big modern colliery plant is a mixture of engineering, carpentering, power, railway, pumping and mining plant. From points miles apart the coal is brought from the face, lifted, sorted, cleaned and finally despatched by rail to the consumer. Great numbers of men are employed, many technical trades are involved, and the whole organization is concentrated in getting and assembling coal from many points with the maximum of speed and the minimum of danger and of cost.

Having left all smoking materials behind—for it is an offence under the Coal Mines Regulation

---

[1] We do not touch upon composite undertakings of which there are many, wherein we have under the same company and general management not only mines but by-product works, and it may be steelworks or brickworks, etc.

A MODERN COLLIERY 55

Act of 1911 to take matches or pipes, etc. into a mine—the first thing to do is to obtain a lamp from the lamp cabin. The lamp cabin is where the hundreds of lamps are kept, examined, cleaned and repaired. It is light work, and men who are injured are frequently given work here. The lamps giving the best light are electric, but the oil lamp is still extensively used owing to the fact that it is impossible[1] to test for gas with an electric lamp.

Armed with the lamp, one next goes to the up-cast shaft and examines the method adopted to keep the top practically air-tight, so that the 400 or 500 h.p. ventilating fan can draw a powerful current of air through the mine by pulling the air up the up-cast shaft and down the down-cast shaft. If the up-cast shaft were open to the air at the top the ventilating fan would, of course, be useless as the air would simply be drawn from outside instead of from below.

The lamp having been examined the visitor then enters the cage, a signal is given to the winding engineman and the cage is lowered at a rate which to the novice appears uncomfortably quick. Assuming the mine is of a normal depth, say two thousand feet, the bottom will be reached in a few seconds and then one steps out, not into black darkness relieved by a flickering light, but into a high-walled corridor lit with electric light along which small coal trams or tubs are running.

[1] Very recent researches indicate the possibility of this disadvantage being overcome.

On one side of the cage these trams are all empties, hurrying back to the coal-face, on the other, they are all full, hastening to the cage to be drawn up to the surface where their contents are tipped into hoppers which feed the screen belts. Both sets of trams are pulled along by an endless steel rope worked by electric haulage gear.

The visitor will next have pointed out the compressed air pipe carrying the compressed air which, in a dangerous mine, is used to work the coal cutters, the water pipe through which water is being pumped from the workings to the sump, i.e. the well at the bottom of the shaft whence it is pumped to the surface by powerful underground electric pumps, and finally to the electric cable carrying the current from the surface to the transformers underground where it is charged from about 2000 volts to some 500 volts. This low-pressure current is then used to drive all the electrical machinery which is situated at the shaft bottom.

The shaft bottom is the name given to an area sometimes three hundred yards square which is solid ground in which the coal is left. The two shafts are sunk and then roadways are driven out in various directions. These roadways are high and wide and are walled in brick. A double line of rails is laid for the trams to run upon and various places are cut out for use as underground offices, power-houses, stables, etc. The whole of the shaft bottom is lit up with electric light except

A MODERN COLLIERY 57

that portion along which the bad air comes from the mine to the up-cast shaft. That part is separated from the rest for safety and ventilation purposes by numerous air-tight doors.

Immediately the pre-arranged limits of the shaft bottom have been reached the miner begins to cut into the coal seam which exists throughout the area forming the pit bottom, but is there left intact as we have said. As he cuts the coal away

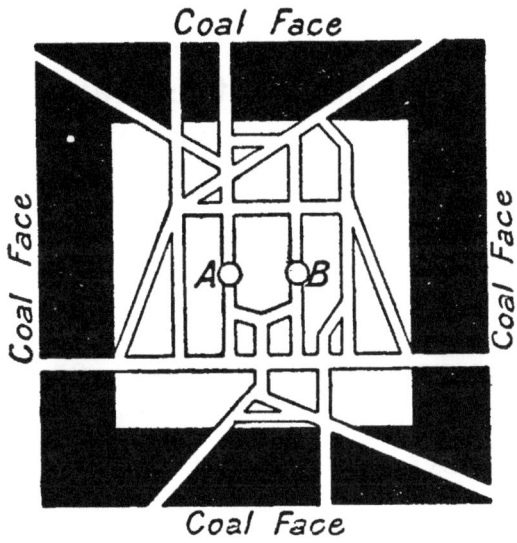

and it is removed a space is formed around the pit bottom which gets wider and wider, and in time the weight of the earth above pressing on this space causes it to close. The miner working at the coal-face would thus find himself cut off from the pit bottom were it not that roadways are kept open for him by means of timbering.

Thus, if the small drawing is followed, it will be seen that the centre white square which represents the shaft bottom is traversed in many directions by roads. These are haulage roads so designed that all the full trams coming from the various workings arrive at the same side of the cage, while all the empty trams emerging from the other side of the cage can be despatched to their various destinations. Outside the white square is a black surround also crossed by roads. These are the main haulage roads. The black portion represents the part from which coal has been got and which has fallen in by pressure from above. That portion will consist of the strata on which the coal rested before it was cut away, rubbish or 'dirt' caused during the cutting of the coal and thrown away by the miner, and the strata which was above the coal and which has now subsided. The whole is called the goaf, or gob, or waste, and it is here that gob fires may arise, or gob stink be generated. The coal-face, at which the men are working, lies beyond the part shaded black. The haulage arrangements at the face are shown in the next diagram.

It will of course be evident that the above figure represents the conditions immediately after the mine has been 'opened out' as it is called. After the miners have been at work a few years a great area of coal will have been removed and the haulage roads will extend for miles.

As we have said, the haulage roads are kept open by timbering. This consists of placing every so often, according to the nature of the 'roof' or

A MODERN COLLIERY

strata above the coal, upright props usually of fir and about a foot in diameter on either side of the passage-way which is to form the road. Stretching across from the top of one prop to the top of the other a beam is then placed and the whole keeps

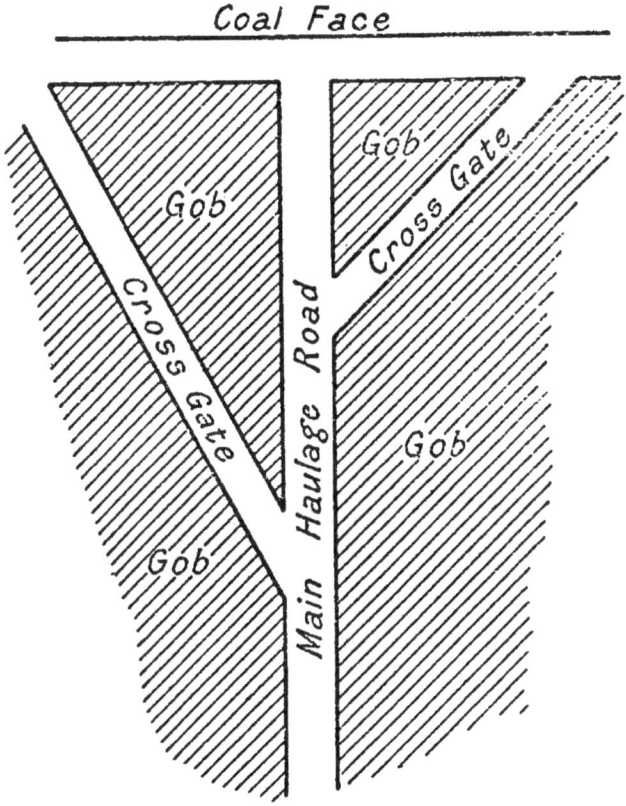

the 'roof' up along the line of the roadway. The pressure is so great that no props however strong could support the weight of the upper strata were it not that the 'waste' on either side enables the weight to be distributed.

Proceeding down the main haulage road along which the trams or tubs are pulled by mechanical haulage we shall see occasionally on either side, as we near the coal-face, hand haulage roads called cross gates down which the coal is hauled from other parts of the coal-face by ponies. The pony-hauled trams, as soon as they reach the main haulage roads, are clipped on to the haulage rope[1] and then dragged along to the pit bottom.

Arrived at the coal-face we find that the miners have divided up the length of the coal-face into divisions called 'stalls,' and at each of these stalls men are at work holing, or firing, and breaking down the coal and filling it into trams which run on rails along the coal-face and are pushed by boys until they get to the haulage roads. In some mines, where the conditions are favourable, the coal is taken from the face to the trams on the haulage roads by mechanical conveyors on the endless belt or shaker systems. American and English practice, however, tends to show that coal conveyors can only be usefully employed where the natural conditions are favourable.

The general principle of coal-getting is based on the fact that it is easier to knock a wall down than it is to cut your way through it. The miner therefore generally cuts away at the bottom of the coal seam, puts an explosive charge in the top and so causes the coal to break down just as if you attacked a jutting-out piece of masonry with a

---

[1] We are, of course, only describing one type of working. Thus the mechanical haulage may be of the main and tail type, and not of the endless rope type described, etc., etc.

A MODERN COLLIERY 61

sledge hammer. The coal is then broken into manageable sizes and filled into the tram. The operation involves the employment of three grades of labour: The collier who does the under holing as it is called and breaks up the coal. The shot-firer who fires the shot. The putter, trammer, or filler who fills the tram and is in a grade lower than the collier.

We will assume that in the mine we are visiting the work of holing is being done by a coal-cutting machine. The collier now does not do the holing by hand but operates the machine, which is either driven by electricity or, in the case of a dangerous mine, i.e. a mine liable to escape of gas from the coal seams, by compressed air. There are, of course, a great number of coal-getting machines, all of which have their several excellences, the percussive for heading, the chain for under-cutting or bottom holing, etc., etc. We can only indicate the general method. This consists in cutting away a space about two inches high and three or four feet deep into the strata below the coal seam throughout its whole length. The machine operated by the collier drags itself along the coal-face by pulling along a chain and makes a clean cut in the desired direction.

Having under-cut the seam, the shots are then fired and quickly the coal wall to the depth cut into by the machine is broken down, the coal broken up, filled and trammed away.

Meanwhile the men are working in front of the

coal-face in a place which, as the face recedes due to the cutting away of the coal, will in time become the gob and will be crushed in by the weight of the strata above except where the haulage roads are kept open. This crushing-in process would commence too soon and the men working be killed or injured were it not that the roof which is slowly settling is kept up for a time with pit props, similar to those used to preserve the haulage roads, only smaller, their use being but temporary. It is greatly to the miner's advantage to make the coal-face travel quickly, as it is called, for then he does not have to work under a roof that has started to settle. Whenever a strike occurs of any duration it is almost always found that this settling process has advanced in places to such an extent that the roof has fallen in, and before work can be resumed it is necessary to clear up the stalls and do a considerable amount of re-timbering.

The cost of timbering is to-day very considerable. Before the war nearly all the timber used in our mines came from abroad, mainly from Scandinavia, France and Portugal. The cost was such in those days that it meant 1d. to 6d. a ton on the cost of coal according to the district and the amount of timbering necessary. As a result of the loss of ship-tonnage during the war and the enormous increase in freights we had to rely very largely on home-grown timber which was inferior in quality and very much higher in price. The result was and is that instead of **1d.** or **6d.** the coal owner has to allow from **1s.** to **2s.** to every ton of coal to meet the cost of timber. In addition to the material cost there has to be added the considerable cost involved in setting the timber and in keeping it repaired and in proper order. This is the work of the underground timberman.

Despite this timbering and the normal careful upkeep of the working places it is necessary in order to preserve safety that before the men can commence work that the districts in which they work should be examined. This is the duty of the class of officials variously described as the examiners, firemen or deputies whose rank is that between the under-manager (who holds a second-class certificate) and the collier. In order that this examination may take place before the men commence their labours it has in the past been considered necessary for the examiner to work longer hours than the men as they must, as we have seen, examine the district of the mine for which they are responsible before work is commenced, and it is considered very desirable for the same examiner to see the men out at the end of the shift so that when the examiner for the following shift came in the two could compare notes and the examiner in the first shift point out danger zones to his colleague.

The duty of examination is not, of course, confined to dangers arising from the roof falling or the floor lifting,[1] but to all other matters which might affect safety, particularly to the existence of a 'blow' of gas or fire-damp or of a gob fire. The fire-damp imprisoned in the coal seams may at any moment be set free by the working in the face or, more usually, may effect its escape during a temporary cessation of operations. It is almost universally the case that a mine is most dangerous after it has been lying idle, and the longer work is suspended the more dangerous it becomes.

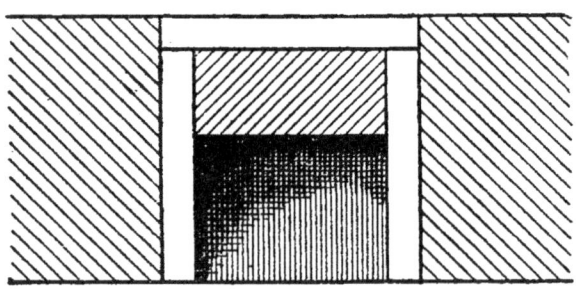

It will be realized from what we have been saying that the height of the haulage roads unless special work was done on them would be the height of the coal seam. In many cases this would be from twenty to thirty inches, which would greatly impede the efficient working of the mine. We remind the reader that in the early days of last century it was a common practice for the women and children who were employed to pull the trams along to crawl along the roads in conse-

[1] The floor may in some cases, e.g. where it is a clay floor, lift very perceptibly in a few hours under the influence of water, and has been known to lift feet in the course of a three weeks' stoppage.

quence of the roof being so low. It will be recalled that in the debate in the House of Lords one of the peers expressed his conviction that women were a necessity in some thin-seam mines for this reason. Modern skill has shown a far better and more efficient way out of the difficulty. The 'roof' immediately above the coal seam at the place where it is intended to have the haulage roads is what is termed 'top ripped.' That is to say, the stonemen cut away the over-lying strata to a sufficient depth so that the roadway is high enough to permit easy passage of men and ponies.

This practice of top ripping has frequently other advantages. It constantly happens that the strata immediately above and in contact with the coal seam is at the point of contact, and for some depth in, extremely friable with the result that it forms a very unsatisfactory roof and could only be kept up by the extensive use of cross timbering. In such cases, quite apart from the advantages flowing from higher roadways, it is economical to cut away the friable part until a sound and strong roof is reached which will not easily fall and which does not require constant support. On the other hand, it occasionally happens that the immediate strata above the coal forms a good roof, but if it were cut away even to the extent of a foot or so, strata would be penetrated into which would not form a roof at all, and consequently, were top ripping resorted to, falls of roof would be continuous and the working of the mine impossible. Such cases are rare, but they do occur, and are the explanation of the excessively low haulage roads which for short distances are sometimes found.

In some of the most modern and best-managed of our collieries the roads are magnificent and are frequently driven specially as roads and quite independent of the coal seam, i.e. they follow a prepared plan and do not conform to the configuration of the seam as they would do if the roads were simply the protected part of the space formed by digging away the coal as above described. Where the roads are specially driven they are frequently almost as straight and the floor as true as that of a light railway.

We have so far described, very shortly and simply, the 'longwall' system of working. There is, however, another method essentially the same so far as the roads are concerned, but different as regards the way in which the coal seam is attacked. This other method, known as the 'bord and pillar' system, consists in heading into the coal seam in parallels, then at a given distance turning to right and left until a pillar of coal is isolated, which pillar is then cut away. It has in our humble opinion many disadvantages over the longwall system, the main drawback consisting in the fact that it involves a considerable amount of 'heading,' i.e. the digging of a tunnel or corridor through the coal, a much more difficult and expensive matter than the breaking down of the undercut coal in the longwall system. In certain

A MODERN COLLIERY

circumstances it is regarded, however, by some experts as having advantages. It is the most ancient of the two methods in existence to-day, being the descendant of the ancient beehive or stoop and room forms of coal mining. In the old days, however, the pillars were much smaller and were left standing for support so that all the coal got was obtained by heading. To-day, of course,

PLAN SHOWING BORD AND PILLAR SYSTEM

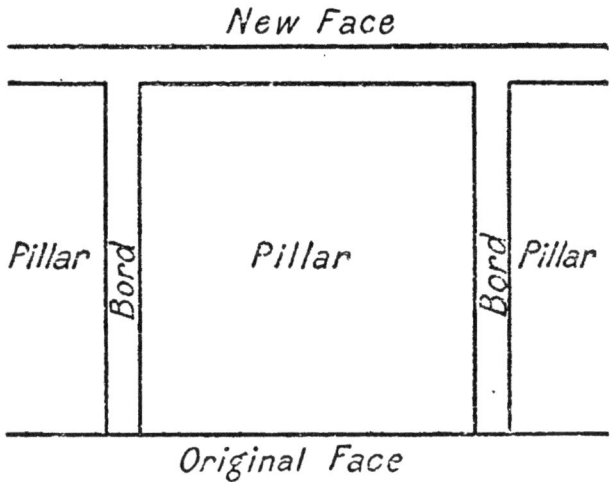

the pillar is cut away, but this, in memory of past practices, is still known as ' robbing.'

The ventilation of mines to-day has reached a very high state of perfection. It would be an exaggeration to say that mines can boast that, like the underground tubes, they are 'cool in summer and warm in winter,' but the ordinary visitor would find that in a modern mine the heat is not oppressive[1] and the quality of the air not

[1] There are occasional hot mines where the working conditions are exceedingly hard. Such cases are, however, the rare exception and not the rule.

noticeably worse than the ordinary atmosphere, though, of course, the heat takes away all sense of freshness. The original draught, as we have seen, is created by a very powerful fan drawing the air up the up-cast shaft through the roadways and workings and down the down-cast shaft from the outside air. The whole system depends upon the simple principle that air will always flow by the shortest route to fill up a partial vacuum, and all that is necessary therefore is to prevent short circuiting in order to cause the air current to penetrate into every part of the pit. This short circuiting is prevented sometimes by air-doors, sometimes by walling and sometimes by brattice cloth.

As the air current is passing down the roadways it is obviously necessary that the obstacles placed to direct the air current and to stop short circuiting shall be so designed that they will not prevent the passage of the tubs, ponies and men. The brattice cloths are consequently cut into strips and hung almost like curtains so that while able to stop the air current and direct it they can easily be passed through by the pit ponies. In the same way the doors are made so that the ponies or tubs by pushing against them can cause them easily to open.

Having now taken a casual look round the underground workings we must return to the surface where the coal that has been got below is being handled, cleaned, sorted and placed in waggons for delivery to the consumer.

A MODERN COLLIERY

The first thing we shall have to notice is the method of clearance at the shaft top. How the tubs arrive in the cage to be hurried along rails into a tipper which receives them one by one and in the course of a few seconds empties the contents of each tub into a shoot which transfers the coal to a endless belt which conveys it to the screens.

The working of the screens is very complex and can only be described here in the most general way. The purpose of screening is to separate the coal into sizes—large coal, nuts, slack, etc.—and also to eliminate as much ' dirt ' or lumps of stone, band, etc. as can be picked out by hand. The purpose of the washing is to eliminate dirt.

In order for the screening process to take place the coal is conveyed on endless belts between rows of boys or women whose duty it is to pick out the big lumps which are thrown into shoots and are conveyed to waiting trucks; the remaining coal then passes between other rows of workers who, as the coal passes by, pick out the pieces of stone and band which experience enables them to recognize very quickly. The work here is laborious and continuous, the pickers having to work, so to speak, against the machine. The smaller coal thus picked is then conveyed on to screens of different sizes. These screens are practically riddles with large meshes and are kept in constant agitation by mechanical means. The coal which does not pass through the screen of a given mesh is conveyed on to the same belt which in turn transports it to a railway truck in which is thus assembled all the coal of approximately the same size. The coal which passes through the screen is conveyed to another screen of a smaller mesh. The coal which remains on that screen is transported to another truck, and the coal which passes through goes to another screen and so on.

In the above description we have assumed that the coal is not being washed, at any rate at the colliery. If it is being washed instead of being conveyed to railway trucks it would pass to conveyors which would take it to the washery. Some washeries not only wash but screen as well.

A washery is a very expensive and elaborate plant but the underlying idea is simplicity itself. It depends on the fact that stone is heavier than coal and that if both are kept agitated in water the stone will sink to the bottom and the coal will remain on top. The result is that by elaborate mechanical devices it is possible practically to eliminate all the stone, etc., from the coal, leaving nothing but fuel for delivery to the consumer.

The saving in transport which would be effected were all the coal in this country to be washed is very remarkable. No precise figures are available but as a rough approximation it may be stated that on the average $1\frac{1}{2}$ per cent of the total coal raised is dirt. Granted therefore an output of 150,000,000 tons of coal per annum, the quantity of dirt which would have to be conveyed to the consumer and away from the consumer (for, of course, dirt does not burn and consequently has to be removed from the fire-place, furnace, etc., when the coal is consumed), were it not specially removed at the colliery, would be 2,500,000 tons annually, or, assuming that the average distance over which coal is transported from colliery to consumer is twenty miles, then no less than 50,000,000 ton miles of railway work would be thrown away in merely conveying dirt to the consumer. To this has to be added the waste of labour involved in disposing of the dirt after the coal that was with it has been burnt.

The proportion of dirt to coal got from any particular working stall depends on many things, but it is of the essence of good coal-getting to keep the proportion as low as possible. Often the natural conditions affect the matter. It may be that in the seam there is a broad band of dirt or stone and in such a case it is not always an easy matter to prevent some of the dirt being filled into the tubs which should contain coal alone; it may be that the method of filling tends to increase the quantity of useless matter filled. Where, however, the proportion of dirt is unduly high it is generally a sign of careless or inexperienced workmanship on the part of the collier, the filler, or both.

It should be most carefully borne in mind that, although there is not a great deal to learn in the craft of the collier, a very considerable amount of practice and experience is necessary before anyone can become really competent. The importance of this point will become apparent when we come to consider some of the causes of reduction of output. It is therefore, as a rule, the aim of good managers to train up the underground workmen so that, beginning as boys, they shall go through all the stages in between door-trapping and coal-getting before they arrive at the top of their ladder and become colliers. Usually a lad will commence at some simple work such as looking after the air-doors, then he will work under a foreman on the haulage roads, then he will go to the working stalls and fill tubs, then he will work actually at the face as a drawer, i.e. he will be employed in clearing the face of the coal got by the collier. Finally he will become a collier. There is thus no question of apprenticeship or long-continued training at the specific trade of coal-getting. As a result it sometimes happens that the workman is far less skilled than he would have been had he been taught his trade by a first-class man. It is a mystery this trade of coal-getting, which is 'picked up' rather than learnt, with the result that in the same mine and in the same district of the same mine it is possible to find working stalls which tell plainly to all who can see and understand, the one that a master workman works there, the other that a careless and incompetent labourer is digging coals for hire.

CHAPTER IV

OUTPUT

WE have given in the preceding chapter such particulars relating to the working of a colliery as are in our opinion absolutely necessary to be known before it is possible to understand the present position as regards output. These particulars have been made as simple and few as possible, because it is not the purpose of this book to explain how coal is got. It is rather one of its purposes to show why so little coal is being got to-day and how by some means or other that low productivity must cease if the nation's industries are ever to regain their pre-war prosperity.

We shall consider the matter from three points of view: (1) loss of output due to loss of time; (2) loss of output due to lack of intensity of effort in the time actually worked; (3) loss of output due to material difficulties and the insufficient use of mechanical appliances. We shall also have occasion to point out the special problems presented by the peculiar circumstances induced by the war which still affect the production of coal, not only in this but in other countries also.

If the Blue Book containing the proceedings before the Coal Industry Commission[1] is consulted it will be found that throughout the year 1917–18 the two most important causes of loss of time were holidays and transport difficulties, the following being the number of days so lost[2]:—

Time Lost Due to Holidays

Four weeks ended	Days lost through holidays	Four weeks ended	Days lost through holidays
28 April, 1917	1,752,200	13 Oct., 1917	58,300
26 May ,,	231,600	10 Nov. ,,	15,400
23 June ,,	1,496,200	8 Dec. ,,	7,500
21 July ,,	648,600	5 Jan., 1918	2,873,300
18 Aug. ,,	1,723,300	2 Feb. ,,	32,500
15 Sept. ,,	125,300	2 March ,,	100
		30 March ,,	780,600

The total of the days so lost throughout the year in respect of holidays was thus 9,744,900. During the period under consideration it is almost exactly correct to say that 974,490 men were, on the average, employed in the industry, so that it is apparent that the holidays taken represent ten days for every man employed. This means that about 9,500,000 tons of coal were lost through

[1] First Stage, Appendix, 22.
[2] In the figures which follow the number of days shown represent men-days, i.e. if 1,000,000 men are idle one day that is shown as 1,000,000 days.

holidays, the average tonnage of coal raised per hundred shifts for the same period being :—

Four weeks ended	Tonnage per 100 shifts worked	Four weeks ended	Tonnage per 100 shifts worked
28 April, 1917	101·3	13 Oct., 1917	98·6
26 May ,,	101·2	10 Nov. ,,	98·7
23 June ,,	99·5	8 Dec. ,,	98·1
21 July ,,	99·6	5 Jan., 1918	96·3
18 Aug. ,,	98·1	2 Feb. ,,	97·5
15 Sept. ,,	98·6	2 March ,,	98·1
		30 March ,,	97·4

The loss of time during the period under review, due to transport difficulties, was as follows :—

TIME LOST DUE TO TRANSPORT DIFFICULTIES

Four weeks ended	Days lost through transport difficulties	Four weeks ended	Days lost through transport difficulties
28 April, 1917	599,100	13 Oct., 1917	1,030,900
26 May ,,	628,000	10 Nov. ,,	1,101,200
23 June ,,	499,200	8 Dec. ,,	1,265,300
21 July ,,	954,800	5 Jan., 1918	804,300
18 Aug. ,,	696,100	2 Feb. ,,	1,416,700
15 Sept. ,,	662,000	2 March ,,	1,116,800
		30 March ,,	626,700

This question of loss of time through transport difficulties requires explanation. It will be seen that from April, 1917, to March, 1918, no fewer than 11,401,100 man-days were lost through this cause, but the occasion was altogether exceptional. The period under review synchronizes with the intensive submarine campaign commenced in the opening months of 1917. As a result of that campaign it frequently happened that ships had to be diverted from the port they were expected at to other ports; on other occasions ships which had been allocated for the export of coal had to be utilized for the conveying of more essential cargoes to replace those lost through submarine activity, etc. As a result the available rolling stock could not be used to the best advantage. Train-loads of coal originally destined, say, for Cardiff had to be diverted to some other port or, having arrived at the first, had to wait there until a ship arrived. As a further result due to this necessary wastage on the part of railway rolling stock carrying space, collieries frequently were without railway waggons.

We now ask the reader to remember what he saw when he went with us to see the colliery screens and the washery. There everything narrowed down to a number of shoots along which the picked or washed coal was passing into railway trucks. If those trucks were not there the whole operation would of necessity have to be terminated. The screens would stop, the washing would stop, winding would stop, except for the purpose of getting the men up, and the pit would cease work for the day. This was what in fact in many cases happened, with the result that every man employed in the industry played in 1917–18, in consequence of this cause alone, some 12 days, or, from the two causes we have so far examined, 22 days.

The period, as we have seen, was altogether abnormal so far as transport difficulties are concerned. Thus in the twelve weeks ended 5th January, 1918, the time lost through this cause was 3·23 days, whereas for the twelve weeks ended 4th January, 1919, it was but 0·09 days. At the same time transport difficulties are, even in peace times, the reason for a certain amount of loss of output. Anything which interferes with the smooth working of the elaborate system necessary to keep our available waggons employed to the maximum tends to aggravate the coal situation. To give an example we may refer to the Nottinghamshire strike which occurred throughout that coalfield in the early months of 1919. The strike was concerned with a number of points the most important of which was the settling of a county day rate for various classes of underground labour; it lasted nearly three weeks and threw some forty thousand men idle. The loss of time so caused would appear under the head of 'disputes,' but apart from the actual wastage due to the dispute there were other results tending to reduce output which were felt long afterwards. At the time of this strike our rolling stock was still barely sufficient for our needs, and rather than allow trucks to remain unused in a strike area where for the time they were unwanted, the available trucks were diverted to other areas. As a result Nottinghamshire suffered from transport difficulties in an aggravated form long after the strike had been settled. Again, when work is suspended there is a tendency, as we have seen, for the roofs to fall in, for the roadways to become defective, etc.; as a result it is some days after men have returned to work before the colliery resumes its normal output.

The loss of time directly due to strikes during the period under review was comparatively small, the figures being as follows :—

Four weeks ended	Days lost through disputes	Four weeks ended	Days lost through disputes
28 April, 1917	26,400	13 Oct., 1917	256,900
26 May ,,	39,400	10 Nov. ,,	492,400
23 June ,,	52,700	8 Dec. ,,	53,900
21 July ,,	92,100	5 Jan., 1918	31,200
18 Aug. ,,	155,200	2 Feb. ,,	71,000
15 Sept. ,,	126,400	2 March ,,	80,200
		30 March ,,	59,100

This total of 1,536,900 days lost through disputes does not, however, take notice of such indirect effects reflecting upon output as we have indicated above. Even so, it represents a loss of about $1\frac{1}{2}$ days for every man in the industry, and this in time of war when, thanks to the wisdom of the

OUTPUT

men's leaders, strikes were officially discouraged. It will be for the reader to decide, after he has considered what we have to say on the machinery for settling disputes, whether in his view this cause of loss of time could, with good will, be entirely avoided without anyone suffering in the slightest degree. It must be borne in mind that a larger district or national stoppage enormously increases the figures. For the year 1919 it is probable that instead of the 1917–18 loss of 1,536,900 days we must expect to find that not less than 15,000,000 days[1] have been thrown away in disputes, even assuming that the closing months of the year are not marked by any serious stoppages.

It is true that the above wastage occurred during a period when nerves were strung to the highest pitch and when industrial unrest was very marked. It must also be remembered, however, that very considerable improvements, both as regards wages and conditions of work, have been conceded. It is therefore a matter for comment that during this period the loss of time due to disputes has not been reduced but is greatly in excess of that suffered from this cause, except in those years when general national stoppages occurred.

When we turn to the next cause of loss of time, 'other causes,' we find some difficulty in determin-

[1] This is probably a substantial underestimate, the loss due to disputes up to the 21st June, 1919, averaging for the whole kingdom 9·02 days for every man employed. The Yorkshire strike took place in July-August.

ing what these other causes are. An examination of the returns from which the statistics are compiled show, however, that the main 'cause' is unofficial holidays which, being unofficial or not customary, are not shown under the heading of 'holidays.' In the period under review the time so lost was as follows :—

Four weeks ended	Time lost through 'other causes'	Four weeks ended	Time lost through 'other causes'
28 April, 1917	158,900	13 Oct., 1917	43,000
26 May ,,	102,600	10 Nov. ,,	30,900
23 June ,,	98,600	8 Dec. ,,	29,000
21 July ,,	96,800	5 Jan., 1918	30,000
18 Aug. ,,	103,800	2 Feb. ,,	51,400
15 Sept. ,,	39,400	2 March ,,	31,000
		30 March ,,	43,000

To this loss of 858,400 days we have finally to add the wastage due to lack of trade, to repairs and accidents, in order to arrive at the grand total of 25,773,000 days lost from all causes during the year 1917–18, or an annual loss of time for every man employed in the industry of 27 days, which gives a working year of 276 days.

Under this head of loss of output, due to loss of time, we thus see that there are four contributing causes, one of which—holidays—may be regarded as a constant which it is neither desirable nor practicable to attempt to alter; one—transport

OUTPUT

difficulties—is a cause which is extrinsic to the coal industry and is largely a matter of the more efficient handling of railway rolling stock ; one—disputes—is mainly within the power of the men to alter for the better ;[1] the fourth group—' other causes,' lack of trade and accidents, etc.—are partly matters for more efficient management to surmount and partly causes of a fortuitous nature which must continue under any system of working. It is probable that under any form of combination, unification, or nationalization, the item shown under the heading ' loss of trade ' could practically be eliminated, always assuming—and it is a large assumption—that the cost of production did not reach a figure so high as to imperil our export trade. If our export trade were lost or seriously affected it would result in a great aggravation of the situation so far as lost time is concerned, for it is impossible to regulate the internal trade so that all the collieries are working full time and all the coal so got is disposed of to inland consumers. It must also be borne in mind that the system of generating electricity in super-power stations is expected and designed to bring about great economies in the use of fuel, with the result that either our inland consumption of coal will be

---

[1] We do not desire to be understood to mean that the men are usually in the wrong on the merits of the disputes that arise, they are mainly responsible for the loss of time because that loss is not due to a dispute but to a strike, and a dispute can be settled, and usually is in the end, by negotiation to the proper conduct of which a strike contributes nothing.

reduced or the relation of power unit used to workmen employed will be increased. In either case there is no reason to believe that it would be possible, granted that the escape valve of overseas trade were shut down, merely to balance production with inland distribution and still keep all the persons at present employed in the industry fully occupied.

In dealing with loss of time we have not taken into account that form of loss of time due to what is called absenteeism. This, however, is another and an increasingly grave cause of low production.

We shall have occasion to point out hereafter that, in addition to loss of output due to lost time, there is also the important factor of intensity of work to be borne in mind. Before, however, we come to consider that, it is desirable to touch upon some of the very special causes due mainly to the war which have during recent years adversely affected production and which operate still to a certain extent.

If what we have said about the working of a modern colliery is borne in mind it will be apparent to the reader that the coal which is got has to pass through the underground roads, often of considerable length, along rails, and in tubs before reaching the cage. The speed with which this transport is done really represents the speed of production, for it is of little avail to hew coal at a greater rate than it can be transported underground.

OUTPUT

The condition therefore of the haulage—or the state of the clearance as it is called—is a most material factor in the efficiency of the mine, and upon it depends the output of coal to a very great extent.

Now good clearance necessitates the doing of a great deal of 'dead work,' i.e. work which is not immediately productive of coal but which absorbs much labour. Thus top ripping and bottom ripping, necessary in many cases to obtain a good straight and high roadway, involves the labour of cutting away a lot of stone or band and the removal of such useless material to the surface. This is absolutely unproductive work so far as the immediate coal output is concerned, but if it is not done the *future* coal output is lower than would otherwise be the case.

If we now cast our minds back to those perilous years 1916, 1917, and 1918 we find hundreds of thousands of men leaving the mines for the Forces, and we find an insistent need for coal for munitions. The result was that labour was scarce and what there was was used as far as possible upon *immediately* productive work. The roads were consequently to some considerable extent neglected and the effect is being felt to-day.

It must not be imagined that the coal owners were acting in any selfish manner in so neglecting this form of development. The capital of a colliery is largely represented by its ungotten mineral. It was therefore to the coal owner's interest to bite into this capital as little as possible during a period when profits were very strictly limited. The coal owners fully realized this, but there is no evidence to show that they acted in this narrow, unpatriotic way. On the contrary during the war period, while profits were limited by the operation of the E.P.D. and the Coal Mines Excess Payment,[1] they diverted labour to win coal rather than do dead work which would not be immediately productive, but which would place them in a position to earn high profits when, as all then believed would be the case, profits were no longer limited, i.e. after the war.

But not only is output adversely affected by the restriction of this particular form of development, it is equally affected by the absence of many other kinds of development. The need for immediate production during the war tended to bring about the winning of the most easily got coal. 'Dead work,' such as driving long drifts through faults, which in normal times would be undertaken and would result in time in fresh coal-faces being opened up, was often not attempted and in fact could not be undertaken without the sanction of the Coal Mines Department. As a result to-day there is considerably less coal-face being worked upon than would otherwise have been the case.

To return to the roads. For speedy clearance to be possible it is necessary not only for the roads to be in good condition but for the rails and rolling

[1] See p. 52.

stock to be well kept up also. This has not been possible during the war years. Steel was short, materials were hardly obtainable, our metals and our woods were required for purposes more immediately connected with the war. What would, in normal times, have become colliery rails became light rails for use behind the lines in France; the steel which in pre-war years would have gone to make colliery tubs was turned into shells. Precisely the same difficulty was experienced by our railways, with the result that they have greatly decreased in efficiency and speed. But in a colliery lack of speed means of necessity reduced output, for other things being equal, if the speed of the tubs on the roads is reduced fewer tubs reach the cage in any given hour.

This lack of material also made itself felt in other directions. Before the war there had been a steady increase in the number of coal-cutters used in collieries, as may be seen from the figures on the next page.

Every effort was made to maintain the rate of increase not without some measure of success as appears from the figures for 1916–18, but the numbers now employed would have been much greater than they are were it not for the great difficulty that was experienced in obtaining deliveries. To-day it is understood that the demand greatly exceeds the supply. The same applies to other kinds of machinery and plant.

To turn from the difficulties due to the abuor-

TABLE SHOWING THE NUMBER OF COAL-CUTTING MACHINES IN USE, THE OUTPUT OF COAL OBTAINED BY MACHINES AND THE OUTPUT PER MACHINE IN THE UNITED KINGDOM IN EACH OF THE YEARS 1903 TO 1918

Year	Number of Each Kind of Machine						TOTAL OUTPUT of coal obtained by Machines	Output per Machine
	Disc	Bar	Chain	Percussive	Rotary Heading	Total		
1903	483	39	25	77	17	643[1]	5,245,578	8158
1904	516	60	34	122	23	755	5,744,044	7608
1905	580	103	51	188	24	946	8,102,197	8565
1906	656	152	37	254	37	1136	10,202,506	8981
1907	802	227	74	364	26	1493	12,877,244	8625
1908	827	261	94	451	26	1659	13,508,510	8143
1909	847	276	100	448	20	1691	13,728,902	8119
1910	930	333	134	556	6	1959	15,747,558	8039
1911	796	391	371	579	9	2146	18,309,269	8532
1912	1103	468	182	680	11	2444	20,053,082	8205
1913	1243	542	250	841	21	2897	24,369,516	8412
1914	1262	585	294	926	26	3093	23,976,367	7752
1915	1224	553	383	908	21	3089	24,087,684	7798
1916	1255	569	520	1095	20	3459	26,303,110	7604
1917	1241	606	722	1209	21	3799	27,626,298	7272
1918	1259	595	791	1373	23	4041	27,322,980	6761

[1] Including two machines, the kind of which is not stated.

OUTPUT

malities of the war period as regards development and material supplies, to the difficulties due to labour conditions, we find that although, to-day, there are 31,000 more men employed in the industry than there were in 1914,[1] yet the men to-day are not, for various reasons over which they have no control, as efficient as were the men who were employed in 1914.

To understand the reason for what we may term this permissible lack of efficiency it is necessary to bear in mind what we have said about the mode of promotion whereby the boy in time becomes the collier. This line of promotion was disturbed by the war, for a very large proportion of the young men, the ' boys ' as they are called in the industry, of 18, 19 and 20 joined the Army. They came, it might be, off the roads, or from the stalls where they were acting at drawers. They left the collieries in great numbers in the early years of the war—for the larger part joined up before the Conscription Acts were passed. They served for years and they then, or such as were left, returned. Nearly one hundred thousand will never return.

To what did they return ? Their old work ? In some cases to their old work, in some cases *to the work they would have had had they never left the pit*. In other words their service in the Forces counted for promotion.

In permitting or assisting in any such arrangement it must be realized that the miners' leaders

[1] The 1919 figures are 1,141,000 ; 1914, 1,110,000.

and the owners acted with the best motives and in the earnest desire to see that the demobilized soldier did not suffer for having served his country, but it must also be realized that such an arrangement meant two things: (1) the replacement of the man who, before the soldier's return, was doing the work, and (2) the doing of the work by an inexperienced man. The result was some ill-feeling and some loss of efficiency and, as a consequence, decline in output.

These, then, are some of the causes tending to a low productivity *to-day*. These causes are war causes due to war conditions and will in time pass away. We turn now, however, to consider another factor to which we have already adverted, viz. lack of intensity of work, a factor of great importance and one which is not governed, save to a small extent, by conditions induced by the war.

It is here that in our opinion we find ourselves faced with the most disquieting facts. If we take the figures for Durham, a coal district where conditions, e.g. hours of labour, etc., have changed as little as anywhere and where the relationship between masters and men are as cordial as in any of our coalfields, we find that from 1879 to 1918 the ' get ' in tons per person employed decreased by no less than 39·85 per cent. During the same period the tonnage per hewers' shift worked has declined from 4·23 to 3·17, a decline of 25·06 per cent. In both cases the change has been gradual and it is impossible to place one's finger on a date.

or a cause, and say then, or for that reason, the reduction occurred.

If, instead of Durham, we take the whole country we find a similar state of affairs. Thus for the years 1913–19 the average output per person employed and the average output per man per shift is as follows :—

Period	Average output per man	Average output per man-shift
1913	259	1·00
1914	218	·98
1915	266	1·02
1916	265	1·00
1917	250	·96
1918	236	·94
First 20 weeks of 1919	218·4	·89

If we regard this war period as exceptional, and take back our figures to the period 1899–1913, we find a reduction in output per person employed of from 314 tons per annum to 262 tons per annum, while during the same period the earnings per annum per person employed increased from £58 to £82, and the pit-head price of coal was raised from 7s. 4·18d. to 10s. 1·52d., an increase due almost entirely to the increased cost of labour, the increase in 'other costs' being only 4·89d. We should remind the reader that by 1918 this pit-head price had jumped to 22s. 4d. and the earnings per person employed to £159,[1] but these rises practically follow the same curve as currency depreciation.

When we compare these figures of output per man with those of other countries, particularly America, the comparison is against us. Thus :—

OUTPUT PER MAN PER DAY AND PER ANNUM
(*America*)

	(a) Bituminous			(b) Anthracite	
Period	Tons per day	Tons per annum	Period	Tons per day	Tons per annum
1907	2·94	687	1907	2·08	457
1908	2·98	575	1908	2·13	427
1909	—	—	1909	—	—
1910	3·09	671	1910	1·94	445
1911	3·12	659	1911	1·90	468
1912	3·29	732	1912	1·88	433
1913	3·22	747	1913	1·80	464
1914	3·31	646	1914	1·84	451
1915	3·49	709	1915	1·96	450
1916	3·48	800	1916	1·93	489

It is, of course, impossible to compare American output per man per annum with British output. In the States the natural conditions are different, the seams are thicker, the coal more easily got, etc. It is to be expected that, granted equally good

[1] To-day from Workmen's Compensation figures it is found to be £181.

management and equally industrious labour, the worker in America would get a much larger output than the worker in this country. Even so, however, it is very disquieting to find that over a period during which natural conditions did not change either in the States or here, the American output per man per day has substantially increased while the British output per man per shift has substantially decreased.

The causes of this deplorable state of affairs are many, but we believe that the main one is to be found in the fact that in this industry the men and the masters do not work in that harmony which is necessary before men can work with a will. We cannot believe that a great body of men have on the average declined in skill and energy from the level reached by their fathers and grandfathers. We cannot believe that the conditions of work are worse for we know them to be far better. The cause is purely psychological and has its roots in antipathy. The industry will never in our opinion return to its former state of efficiency, so far as the workers are concerned, until the state of antagonism which undoubtedly exists to-day, if not between the rank and file of the men at least between their leaders and the owning class, is eliminated.

It may be argued that the decline in productivity per man employed is due to the fact that as our mines become older and our best seams worked out such a decline is bound to occur. Such an argument is vitiated by the fact that improvements in the method of getting coal have during the last forty years far more than balanced the difficulty of getting the coal. It is destroyed by the further fact that in our new and favourable coalfields, such as the South Yorkshire area, the men working under the most favourable modern conditions and in new mines where the face is near the shaft do not obtain as much coal per man employed as that got by the miners in the country generally under the conditions appertaining forty and fifty years ago.

This leads us to a generalization which we put forward for the reader's acceptance or rejection as he thinks fit. In the old days when the bowls were all biased in favour of the employer, when labour was cheap and its conditions appalling, coal could be got and sold without the master having to take thought how to effect this or that economy and this or that improvement. As a result management was slack, the industry lived on the muscles, and upon the lives, of the workers. To-day, when powerful Unions can exert immense pressure, there is a tendency for matters to be reversed. Now it is for the management continually to work out how to produce coal at a marketable price—the export market being the ultimate test—with the present high wage item, an item which is high not merely because wages are high but also because it requires more men than formerly to produce the same result. A time will undoubtedly come, if it has not already arrived, when this problem will become insoluble, when it will no longer be possible by improvements in management to make up for decline in productivity. When that time arrives one or two things is bound to happen—unless the country is prepared to permit this vital industry to live on charity and become the subject of State doles or subsidies—wages must come down or productivity must go up.

This, then, brings us to the kernel of the matter. Can management be improved, or must the men be looked to to place the industry on a sound economic basis ? Is it probable that State ownership will tend to improve the technique of management ? Is it likely that the men as Government employees will work better and harder or at a lower wage ?

We do not desire to suggest the answers to these questions. We do suggest, however, that there is a problem which must be solved and which does not permit of the continuance of the present state of affairs. It is idle to argue that the condition of the industry is satisfactory and that matters should remain as they are. It is useless to blame the management which is as able as that of any other industry. It is a waste of energy to throw stones at the men and denounce them and their leaders for being antipathetic towards the owners, for they are and will remain so unless and until it is possible to remove the root cause of that antipathy. It is of no purpose to fling the accustomed jibe at bureaucratic management, for no one has suggested that this complex industry should be managed from Whitehall. Granted, and it is a postulate we are very loth to make, that it is impossible to get labour and capital in this industry to work in amity and as colleagues, then we are inevitably presented with an alternative of evils : on the one hand strikes, disputes, restriction of output, intentional or unintentional; on the other hand the elimination of discord by the removal of one of the disputants, an elimination which *if it results in a reduction in the efficiency of management* will, as we have seen, bring down wages or increase the hours or the intensity of work. It cannot, indeed, in our opinion, be doubted that if a modification of the present system of management results in less efficient management, the blow will fall most heavily upon the workers themselves, and this blow will be delivered by a hand—that of Economic Necessity—against which it is useless to appeal.

The above, however, only follows granted the postulate that it is necessary, in order to persuade the men to work with a will, to eliminate one of the two sides—the owners. Many people are unable to see that this necessity exists. The owners, not unnaturally, protest that it is possible to elaborate a system whereby capital and labour can continue to live together and in amity instead of in discord. From time to time proposals have been put forward with this aim. Sir George Elliot proposed one scheme, **Mr. D. A.** Thomas, as he then was, put forward another. Only recently Mr. Frederick Mills propounded a method of co-operative working, and many other proposals have also been advocated and considered with a view to bringing about a *nexus* between labour and capital. We do not propose to examine these schemes, for they have not succeeded in winning acceptance or in solving the problem. We must, however, refer to the proposals put forward by what we must term the employers' representatives on the Coal Industry Commission. They recommended that the following procedure should be established :—

" (1) *Pit Committees.*

There should be established at each colliery a Pit Committee, consisting of equal numbers of representatives of the management and of the mine workers. The numbers will probably vary in the different mines, but in no case should they exceed seven on each side. Each side should have it own Chairman. The representatives of the mine workers should be appointed by and from all the workers employed at the colliery.

The Committee should meet as occasion demands, but not less frequently than once a month, for the consideration of questions of which previous notice has, if possible, been given.

The purpose of the Pit Committee is to afford an opportunity of discussion of any question relating to the working of the mine, or the conditions under which the miners work, and any other questions in the settlement of which both parties are directly concerned.

It is hoped that through personal touch at the mine and free and friendly interchange of views harmonious relations will be promoted and maintained.

(2) *District Councils.*

District councils, consisting of representatives of the coal owners and representatives of the Trade Unions in the district, should be established for the purpose of dealing with any questions of a district character which, in the opinion of the Council, it is in the mutual interest of the parties to discuss. The District Council should also deal with questions of which a settlement has not been arrived at by the Pit Committee.

Where Conciliation Boards exist for the purpose of dealing with questions on a district basis, the procedure of the Conciliation Board and the District Council might with advantage be co-ordinated, or the Conciliation Board might act as the District Council for the district.

(3) *National Council.*

A National Council should be established, consisting of the representatives of mine owners and mine workers appointed by the districts, for the purpose of dealing with any question of national interest which may be referred to it."

This scheme appears to be an elaboration of the Conciliation machinery at present in existence by the super-imposition of committees similar to the Whitley Councils and the Joint Industrial National Council. It does not attack the wider problem which springs from the reluctance of men to work for the gain of another, a problem which is by no means peculiar to the coal-mining industry and which, if accepted as a true and valid difficulty, tends to strike at the capitalistic system altogether. The scheme put forward on behalf of the Mining Association of Great Britain recognized the problem but sought to prove that the difficulty was not a valid one, being based on a misconception of economic laws. It was therefore suggested that the similarity of interest of labour and capital should be brought home to the worker by making wages fluctuate, not, as in the past, mainly with selling prices, but partly with selling prices, partly with cost of production and partly with profits. The intention was probably to reconcile the worker to high profits by showing him—by throwing open for examination all cost accounts—that his interest and the masters' interest was the same because the higher the profit the higher could the wages be.

In Sir Arthur Duckham's words: " The failure to include workmen's representatives on the Board of Directors as a necessary adjunct to the scheme render the main proposals unacceptable." The men indeed want in industry what already exists in the political world—democratic management.

An attempt is made to achieve this result by Sir Arthur Duckham who recommends that the industry shall be controlled by Boards of Management whereon the workmen as well as the management shall be represented.

Though we do not pretend to any knowledge of the inner reasons for the various reports issued by the Coal Industry Commission, it would seem that the position can be summed up as follows :—

All realized that willing and efficient work would not be forthcoming until the men were in a more contented frame of mind. Those who decided for nationalization appear to have believed that no *rapprochement* between the men and the owners was possible, and decided therefore to eliminate one of the sides in the hope and expectation that the men would develop a spirit of citizenship which would cause them to work willingly and hard for the good of the country, and in the knowledge that by so doing they were not in effect increasing the wealth of a class they did not admire and who in their view did less, far less, for the industry in lending their money than the men who worked in it did in spending their lives. Those who decided for the full retention of private ownership and control attempted a *rapprochement* with labour by holding out the inducement of higher wages in the event of profits increasing, they also invited the co-operation of the workers by suggesting the establishment of committees at which the workers could urge changes which, in their view, would make for the better and smoother running of the industry. The workers' powers would thus be advisory and in no way executive. The one member of the Commission who reported in favour of the retention of unified private ownership with joint control would appear to have sought after a reconciliation by giving to the workers executive power. That is to say, *he* regarded the problem as founded on a desire on the part of the worker to have a voice in the working out of his own destiny and he gave him that voice.

We now know that the last of these alternatives is the one which has been most favourably considered by the Government. It remains to be seen whether it will succeed in solving the problem. One thing at least is clear, all the schemes without exception are based on the desire to increase production by creating willing, in the place of unwilling, workers. If that is not achieved then the *raison d'être* of all the schemes, so far as they are concerned with the labour point of view, disappears, and with that disappearance escapes also the last possibility of permanently continuing the present rate of wages and the present hours without further increasing the present price of coal. We shall have occasion hereafter to see how even the existing cost of coal affects the industries of this country.

CHAPTER V

ENQUIRIES AND EXPERIENCES

IT is a little difficult to know to what extent we may now rely upon past experiences in matters relating to fundamental social problems. In the words of the majority of the Commissioners who composed the Union of South Africa State Mining Commissions of 1917: " At the present hour, political thought is dominated by the facility with which States, in pursuit of divers State interests, sacrifice the lives, the property and the well-being of their subjects. The manifestation during the war of the omnipotence of States over their subjects was frequently referred to in evidence as pointing to the necessity of States exercising similarly extensive activity in the time of peace for the purpose of industrial development."

" Several witnesses expressed their belief that as a result of the war humanity generally, and economic institutions in particular, would undergo a drastic change. It is hard to say whether any change is pending, and it is difficult to prophesy what direction the change may take. There may be an expansion of governmental activities in the pursuit of wealth, or there may be a revulsion against the power of Governments over the lives and liberties of individuals. It was frequently asserted in evidence that the exigencies of warfare had settled once and for all the question as to the respective advantages and disadvantages of public and private enterprise. The measures adopted by Governments in industrial organization to secure material for military purposes were accepted as marking the close of the era of industrial organization under the control of the private firm, or the public company. To many witnesses, however, the adoption by the State of the control of certain industries and employments did not afford a solution of the industrial question."

The main objective of the Union of South Africa Labour Party in pressing for the Nationalization of Mines was the reduction of taxation by obtaining profits for the State rather than for private persons. When, however, we turn to Germany, who has its State mines, we find the very well-known expert, Dr. Jüngst, of Essen, saying: " I will sum up my remarks as follows : The capital invested per ton in the State mines on the Saar is considerably less than in the private mines on the Kuhr, but, on the other hand, the surplus profit in the latter is larger than in the former."

If indeed we take as our test past experiences or previous enquiries we shall find a mass of evidence either neutral or directly opposed to State interference. Thus the Belgian Government in reply to the *questionnaire*, " Has the question of State

Mining ever been considered by your State, and if it was not adopted, what consideration prevented your State from embarking on State Mining?" replied: "The considerations which have restrained Parliament from going in for State Mining are chiefly due to the fact that the running of industries by the State is rarely accomplished under advantageous conditions, and that it is in the interest of the nation that mineral resources should be developed in the most economical way."

This reply, given in 1917, may be regarded as the absolute antithesis to the theories of the supporters of nationalization who claim that the industrial machine would work most smoothly under State control and that the State would develop its natural resources in the most economical way. It is in conflict with the views of those new countries which, far freer than European countries from the shackles of the past, have been able to test political theories without incurring the same risk of disaster as might be run were older countries to attempt the same experiments.

Even so, the results achieved in New Zealand, Queensland, Tasmania, South Australia, New South Wales and Victoria, where State coal mines exist, are negative rather than positive in quality. In New Zealand the reasons that induced the State to embark upon coal mining were partly political, partly financial, partly economic and partly experimental. "The political reason may be stated as a popular demand for a State coal mine.

ENQUIRIES & EXPERIENCES 103

The economic reason was the high and rising price of coal. The State mines were started with the intention not only of lessening the cost of coal to the general public, but also of ensuring a regular and cheap supply of coal to the State railways. This latter object may perhaps be regarded as financial."[1]

According to the New Zealand Government's report, after fifteen years' experience, it was found that "the greatest difficulty in connection with State Mining is the labour question." In answer to the question, "Is an extension of State Mining justified?" the answer was, "Provided labour troubles do not increase in intensity, an extension of State Coal enterprise is likely to be successful."

On the other hand, Victoria opened its one State mine in 1909 chiefly owing to a strike which occurred in a neighbouring State, from which the bulk of the coal supply was obtained. That mine has been carried on at a profit, but the Government showed, in 1917, no desire to create further State mines.

These examples of State coal mining do not, however, in our opinion carry us very far. We may consider the results achieved in Queensland to be extremely favourable without in any way confusing the question of nationalization of mines in this, or in any other European, country with complex financial systems and enormous and

[1] State Mining Commission, 1916–17, U.G., 6–17; Minutes of Proceedings, etc., p. 690.

interwoven industries. Queensland, for example, has a coal-mining industry that is absolutely in its infancy and it is almost ridiculous to compare a country whose total wage bill in respect of coal mining is under £1,000 with the United Kingdom having a wage bill of not less than £160,000,000.

Were the results achieved in Australia overwhelmingly against or in favour of nationalization we might be able, despite the difference in the size of the concerns that we should be comparing, to derive much useful conclusions from the experiences of our friends in the Antipodes. Their results, however, as we have suggested, are colourless. The same may be said of Holland which owns four mines. It is therefore more useful to turn to the consideration of State mines in Germany.

State coal mines have existed in Germany for a great number of years, and so far as the important Prussian mining industry is concerned are based on the regalian rights by virtue of which the State was given the right to carry on mining and to reserve certain fields and districts for that purpose. The Silesian State coal mining industry, on the other hand, was begun by Frederick the Great, who established coal-mining operations in order to supply the State smelting works with coke. The very valuable Saar mines passed to Prussia and were operated as State mines as a result of the Peace of Vienna in 1815.

If we consider the development of the Prussian, Upper Silesian, Saar and Westphalian coalfields

ENQUIRIES & EXPERIENCES

under State ownership during the years 1880-1912, and compare those figures with the development of the operations under private control in Germany and in this country, we shall have some useful comparative data on which to base our calculations of the probable future of the industry in this country should it be nationalized under any system similar to that which has existed in Germany.[1]

PRUSSIA

Year	No. of pits worked	Coal Output		Average Number of Employees
		Quantity in tons	Value in Mk. 1000	
1880	18	7,652,494	50,563	31,787
1885	18	9,756,784	61,642	38,298
1890	18	10,590,981	97,387	43,877
1895	17	11,737,375	91,351	46,996
1900	17	15,469,593	162,207	60,338
1901	17	15,121,989	167,135	62,079
1902	20	15,781,187	163,957	64,193
1903	20	16,390,394	168,082	67,523
1904	21	17,206,328	178,241	70,114
1905	21	17,873,588	185,222	71,947
1906	21	18,388,883	198,040	75,517
1907	21	18,523,275	212,025	79,159
1908	22	19,080,126	224,415	83,391
1909	22	19,708,974	224,903	88,721
1910	23	20,634,816	230,053	91,671
1911	23	21,890,307	235,020	92,440

[1] The following tables relating to German mines is from *Glückauf*, Dec. 13th, 1913.

Upper Silesia

Year	Coal Output		Average Number of Employees
	Quantity in tons	Value in Mk. 1000	
1870	1,442,202	7,393	4,983
1875	1,860,435	12,592	6,300
1880	2,086,509	8,663	5,947
1885	3,238,657	13,436	9,175
1890	3,729,583	23,673	12,097
1895	4,177,872	24,065	12,135
1900	5,292,755	40,978	14,993
1901	5,141,372	43,540	15,448
1902	5,211,625	42,981	15,664
1903	5,103,323	40,699	16,394
1904	5,368,340	41,882	17,288
1905	5,541,094	43,473	17,368
1906	5,834,026	48,972	18,086
1907	5,861,737	54,785	19,139
1908	5,882,683	58,384	19,736
1909	6,025,141	58,305	22,000
1910	6,141,114	58,480	22,745
1911	6,337,213	59,037	22,828

Saar District

Year	Coal output in tons	Employees	Year	Coal output in tons	Employees
1870	2,734,019	15,662	1903	10,067,337	43,811
1875	4,481,839	22,902	1904	10,363,720	44,949
1880	5,211,389	22,918	1905	10,638,560	45,737
1885	6,049,031	26,435	1906	11,131,381	47,891
1890	6,212,540	27,528	1907	10,693,214	48,895
1895	6,886,098	30,531	1908	11,070,647	49,998
1900	9,397,253	40,303	1909	11,063,637	51,788
1901	9,376,023	41,923	1910	10,823,483	52,397
1902	9,493,667	42,036	1911	11,458,920	51,736
			1912	11,663,118	48,918

Westphalia

Year	No. of Mines	Coal	Output of Coke	Briquettes	No. of Employees
1902	2	287,806	—	—	2,105
1903	2	449,842	—	20,601	2,674
1904	2	720,022	—	25,349	3,454
1905	4	839,250	—	31,924	4,151
1906	4	972,983	—	31,146	4,686
1907	4	1,046,450	—	31,667	5,745
1908	4	1,310,976	25,997	33,971	7,634
1909	4	1,746,149	219,948	33,371	9,584
1910	3	2,310,102	410,069	34,280	11,136
1911	4	2,814,740	588,416	37,475	13,137
1912	5	3,553,972	930,711	38,355	15,638

Comparing the results achieved under State ownership in Germany and under private ownership in Germany as regards output, and bearing in mind Dr. Jüngst's dictum that " a comparison between the size of a mine and the output per man shows that up to a point the larger mines show a higher man-output per annum, and we would therefore expect State mines to show a higher man-output. The reverse is, however, the case"; we obtain the following tables:—

DEVELOPMENT OF MAN-OUTPUT AND TON-COST IN GERMAN COAL MINES

Year	Yearly Output per Employee			Cost of One Ton Coal		
	Private Mines Tons	State Mines Tons	All Mines Tons	Private Mines Marks	State Mines Marks	All Mines Marks
1881	267	239	261	4·88	6·61	5·18
1882	271	246	266	4·85	6·54	5·14
1883	273	254	270	4·96	6·60	5·25
1884	270	250	267	4·94	6·55	5·22
1885	269	255	267	4·92	6·42	5·19
1886	271	248	267	4·93	6·35	5·18
1887	283	253	278	4·93	6·27	5·16
1888	295	266	290	5·00	6·31	5·22
1889	286	255	281	5·50	6·83	5·72
1890	273	244	268	7·39	9·04	7·66
1891	265	239	260	7·80	9·04	8·00
1892	252	223	247	7·15	8·67	7·38
1893	258	233	254	6·53	8·03	6·75
1894	260	235	256	6·42	7·80	6·63
1895	264	240	260	6·62	7·83	6·81
1896	274	253	271	6·74	7·89	6·92
1897	274	255	271	6·94	8·16	7·13
1898	271	260	269	7·19	8·37	7·37
1899	271	254	268	7·55	8·96	7·77
1900	266	256	264	8·59	10·29	8·84
1901	242	245	242	9·03	11·19	9·35
1902	238	242	238	8·56	10·48	8·84

	Yearly Output per Employee			Cost of One Ton Coal		
Year	Private Mines Tons	State Mines Tons	All Mines Tons	Private Mines Marks	State Mines Marks	All Mines Marks
1903	250	240	248	8·34	10·26	8·62
1904	247	240	246	8·25	10·33	8·56
1905	247	242	246	8·36	10·33	8·66
1906	273	245	268	8·66	10·59	8·93
1907	268	231	263	9·49	11·33	9·74
1908	253	229	250	10·09	11·68	10·31
1909	246	221	243	10·01	11·45	10·21
1910	251	218	246	9·79	11·23	9·99
1911	261	229	256	9·63	10·71	9·78

AVERAGE OF QUINQUENNIAL PERIODS

	Yearly Output per Employee			Cost of One Ton Coal		
Years	Private Mines Tons	State Mines Tons	All Mines Tons	Private Mines Marks	State Mines Marks	All Mines Marks
1881–1885	270	249	266	4·91	6·54	5·20
1886–1890	282	253	277	5·55	6·96	5·79
1891–1895	260	234	255	6·90	8·27	7·11
1896–1900	271	256	269	7·40	8·73	7·61
1901–1905	245	242	244	8·51	10·52	8·81
1906–1910	258	229	254	9·61	11·26	9·84

The above tables in conjunction with the following one give a fairly complete comparison between the achievement in Germany of private ownership on the one hand and State ownership on the other hand.

Development of State and Private Mines in Germany
Average of Quinquennial Periods

Year	No. of Mines	Employees	Output 1000 tons	Output Per cent of total	Value 1000 Marks
Mines in Private Ownership					
1881–1885	459	166,114	44,865	82·38	220,337
1886–1890	403	190,294	53.581	83·37	300,433
1891–1895	364	244,500	63,534	84·75	438,003
1896–1900	311	302,350	81,925	84·64	610,868
1901–1905	306	400,050	97,870	85·14	831,444
1906–1910	289	488,694	125,916	86·29	1,212,078
Mines in State Ownership					
1881–1885	25	38,551	9,596	17·62	62,755
1886–1890	25	42,270	10,691	16·63	74,765
1891–1895	24	48,867	11,436	15·25	94,574
1896–1900	22	58,180	14,872	15·36	130,664
1901–1905	23	70,631	17,083	14·86	179,509
1906–1910	26	87,661	20,002	13·71	225,235
All Coal Mines in Germany					
1881–1885	484	204,665	54,461	—	283,092
1886–1890	428	232,564	64,271	—	375,198
1891–1895	387	293,368	74,970	—	532,577
1896–1900	333	360,530	96,797	—	741,532
1901–1905	327	470,681	114,953	—	1,010,953
1906–1910	315	576,355	145,918	—	1,437,313

The above may be compared with the following relating to the British coal-mining industry.

Development of British Coal-mining Industry Under Private Ownership from 1889–1918[1]

Period	Tonnage raised (Millions)	Value at Pit-head per ton raised s. d.	Profits and Royalties Amount (Mil'ns) £	Profits and Royalties Per ton raised s. d.	Cost per ton raised excluding Royalties — Wages s. d.	Cost per ton raised excluding Royalties — Other costs s. d.	Cost per ton raised excluding Royalties — Total s. d.	Persons employed	Get per person employed Tons	Earnings per annum per person employed £
Average—										
1889 to 1893	178·0	7 4·18	11·7	1 3·78	4 7·16	1 5·24	6 0·40	631,600	282	58
1894 to 1898	195·5	6 2·16	8·7	0 10·68	—	—	—	680,800	286	—
1899 to 1903	224·3	8 8·76	19·2	1 8·54	5 5·52	1 6·70	7 0·22	776,680	288	35
1904 to 1908	249·8	7 10·94	17·2	1 4·52	—	—	—	881,800	283	—
Year—										
1907	267·8	9 0	24·4	1 9·86	—	—	—	925,097	289	—
1908	261·5	8 11	22·7	1 8·83	—	—	—	972,232	269	—
1909	263·8	8 1	14·9	1 1·55	—	—	—	992,333	266	—
1910	264·4	8 2·25	15·9	1 2·43	—	—	—	1,027,339	257	—
1911	271·9	8 2·00	15·3	1 1·50	—	—	—	1,045,272	260	—
1912	260·4	9 1·00	21·2	1 7·54	—	—	—	1,068,751	243	—
1913	287·4	10 1·52	28·0	1 11·38	6 4·01	1 10·13	8 2·18	1,110,884	259	82
1914	265·7	9 11·79	21·5	1 7·42	6 2·92	2 1·45	8 4·37	1,054,105	252	79
1915	253·2	12 5·60	27·4	2 1·97	7 9·58	2 6·05	10 3·63	939,604	270	105
1916	256·4	15 7·24	43·8	3 5·00	9 9·12	2 5·12	12 2·24	984,796	260	127
1917	248·5	16 8·69	33·7	2 8·55	10 5·53	3 6·61	14 0·14	1,006,299	247	129
1918[2]	227·5	22 4·00	35·5	3 1·50	13 2·80	4 3·20	17 6·00	948,000	240	159

[1] Coal Industry Commission Blue Book Appendices to Stage I, Appendix 5, Table I.
[2] Estimated from the information relating to January—September, 1918.

We thus see that as regards what we consider the critical test, output per man, the following shows the position :—

OUTPUT PER MAN PER ANNUM

Average	British (pte. o.)	Germany (pte. o.)	Germany (State o.)
1889–1893	282	247	239
1894–1898	286	249	249
1899–1903	288	254	247
1904–1908	283	258	237
1909–1911	261	253	223

From this we see that, as in the case of America, the productivity per man under private ownership in Germany has gone up, but in Germany, unlike America, the increase is very small, i.e. from 247 to 253. On the other hand, productivity under private ownership in England[1] and under State ownership in Germany has gone down. It has gone down in England from 282 to 261 and from 239 to 223 in Germany. Prior to the passing of the Eight Hours Act it was tending to increase.

If it is argued that apart from the triennial period, 1909–11, productivity was practically constant in this country, an answer may be found in the full table given on page 111, from which it will be seen that after 1911 the reduction, except

---

[1] It should be borne in mind that the hours of labour in British coal mines were reduced in 1908 by the passing of the Eight Hours Act.

ENQUIRIES & EXPERIENCES

for the years 1915, 1916, was considerable. For the first twenty weeks of 1919 the output per man was only at the rate of 218·4 tons per annum. We have intentionally excluded the strike year 1912 and the war years 1914–19 because they are abnormal.

It appears to follow from these figures that, granted natural conditions equal as between State-owned and privately-owned mines in Germany, or, if different, that the difference over the period taken was constant, the tendency towards reduction in output was better checked in the privately-owned mines than in the State-owned mines. From this the presumption appears to be raised that if the German form of State ownership had been in operation in this country over the period taken, the reduction in output, which has in fact taken place under private ownership, would have been still more serious.

Our facts here are ascertained and correct, our arguments are for the reader to consider. If the arguments are sound and the conclusion correct, it is in our opinion a strong point against the German form of nationalization, for it is, as we have shown in a former part of this book, impossible to improve conditions of labour unless productivity or wage cost is increased or reduced respectively.

The whole question of the socialization of the German mining industry has recently been the subject of enquiry in Germany. Unfortunately the question of whether the efficiency of the worker was greater under State ownership than private ownership was left unanswered, and the commissioners were not unanimous in their final conclusions, but they committed themselves to the following views which were held unanimously.[1]

" [The Commission] held unanimously the view that the entire management of the mines by the State on the ordinary bureaucratic lines would seriously interfere with their economic exploitation. Every extension of State undertakings was uneconomic, and therefore to be negatived so long as this economic activity of the State was in any way connected with its political and administrative functions, and unless the bureaucratic tradition was entirely abandoned. The proceedings of the Commission has shown, while admitting all the advantages of the State control of mining, such startling examples of the inadequacy of this cumbrous State organism that there cannot exist a particle of doubt as to the necessity of a radical change."

The Commissioners proceeded to indicate in words which could be applied to our own Departmental system the various drawbacks inherent in attempting to run an industry with the mechanism of a Government Department. We do not consider it necessary to go into details on this point because, as we have already indicated, nobody has proposed to manage the mines in this country on bureaucratic lines.

[1] See the Economic Supplement to the *Review of the Foreign Press*, March 26th, 1919, p. 377.

Apart, however, from the difficulties which the German Commission felt would arise from State control of the old-fashioned type, all the members were unanimous upon another point which it is of great importance to bear in mind, viz. that the separate nationalization of mining, while the capitalistic system continues in other economic spheres, " cannot be regarded as socialization, but merely as the substitution of one employer for another."

We have little doubt that, whether this is sound or unsound, it would be strongly urged as a reason for extending the principle of nationalization to other industries if those industries to which it had been applied proved failures. This apparent paradox would follow, we believe, from the allegation that the failure was not due to the nationalization of one but to the non-nationalization of the others. On the other hand, if nationalization were a success, its extension would be irresistibly pressed. It therefore appears to us that although the coal industry is made the battling-ground every other industry sooner or later would be affected by the result.

It seems almost to be beyond question that if any form of nationalization were decided upon which resulted in our mines being controlled in the same way as were the German State-owned mines, then, in the words of Sir. F. Oppenheimer, " all industries using coal (and which do not ?) will find that the price of coal will range higher after [such] nationalization than before. The increase in the cost of production, serious in itself, will be accompanied, if the lesson from the Saar counts for anything, by a bad quality, an unreliable supply and a delay in its delivery."[1]

This dictum, however, although very decidedly against nationalization of the German type, does not conclude the matter. It may be possible to develop a scheme that avoids many of the defects of the old German system but which yet retains the essence of State ownership. We believe that the Chairman's Report contains such a scheme, and if this be so we are left once again without guidance from the experiences of others, for they have experienced the effects of a quite different kind of nationalization, viz. a nationalization in which the industry's finances are bound up with the national budget, a nationalization in which management is largely bureaucratic and in which the working of the industry is very liable to political influences. That such a system would fail might have been prophesied, that the failure was only partial is rather a matter for surprise.

To sum up : we find that so far as Australasia is concerned the deductions to be drawn from their experience of nationalization are neutral, their experience is also hardly valuable to us as their coal-mining industry is in each case but yet in its infancy and is a matter which calls for no highly developed organism for its management or working.

[1] U.G., 6-17, p. 725.

ENQUIRIES & EXPERIENCES

We find that Belgium, having enquired into the matter, is opposed to nationalization, and if we perused the Blue Book of the Union of South Africa State Commission we should find that South Africa, after enquiry, had come to the same conclusion. From the same source we find that the experience of the Netherlands shows that State-owned[1] coal mines give results similar to those attained by privately-owned coal mines. Turning to the most important case of State-owned mines —that of Germany—we find that the results obtained do not compare favourably with those reached in the same country under private enterprise, but that the conclusions that may be based thereon are largely vitiated by the fact that the system of State control adopted by the German State is one which is not likely to give satisfactory results, and could, when working out a new organization, undoubtedly be improved upon.

These may be regarded as negative conclusions which are not helpful. They have, however, their uses. They show, on the one hand, that we should be chary of accepting arguments based on the experience of those countries whose coal industry is a very small matter and, on the other hand, of being prejudiced against any form of nationalization by reason of the comparatively bad results attained in Germany under an imperfect system of State management. The German experiences also help us to see more clearly what

[1] There are only four State-owned coal mines in Holland.

to avoid—if such things can be avoided under nationalization, i.e. the mingling of the industry's finances with the State finances, the subjecting of the industry to political influences, the managing of the industry under a bureaucratic system.

An attempt is made to escape the first of these disadvantages by Clause lxxv of the Chairman's report which provides as follows :—

"The Treasury shall not be entitled to interfere with or to have any control over the appropriation of moneys derived from the industry. The said moneys shall be kept entirely separate and apart from other national moneys."

There can be no doubt that this is a vital clause and that any system which was dependent on Treasury control would be doomed to failure, not because the Treasury are dilatory or inert, they may be extraordinarily expeditious and energetic, but because any such control would immediately open the way to bureaucratic management and would subject the industry to the sharpest political pressure.

The last of the above-mentioned weaknesses inherent in the German system is struck at in the Chairman's scheme for managing the industry largely by means of the existing management, the Board of Directorate being replaced by various Councils representative of the four parties mainly interested—the management, the men, the consumer and the State. It is further attacked by Clause lxxvi which provides as follows :—

ENQUIRIES & EXPERIENCES 119

"It being of vital importance that the Mines Department should be managed with the freedom of a private business, the present Civil Service system of selection and promotion by length of service, of grades of servants, of minuting opinions and reports from one servant to another, and of salaries and pensions, shall not apply to the servants attached to the Mines Department."

The third of the above-mentioned defects—political pressure—creates, however, an extremely difficult problem, a perfect solution of which has yet to be propounded. Political pressure, as we see the matter, may be exercised in either of two ways. The industry, if a State industry, would be in such a position that it would tend to become a political object. That is to say, a politician desirous of attracting the large number of votes possessed by miners would perhaps hold out promises relative to the conditions under which the industry would be run in future, promises which could be made in the case of a State concern but which would not be so available as political capital were the control of the industry in private hands.

In so far as such promises were made in the sure knowledge that the resulting changes would be for the benefit of the country as a whole, and not merely of the coal industry, no one need fear such political interference; it is obvious, however, that, without sinking to the level of those for whom the word politician is a word of offence, such promises would be made in hope rather than in sure knowledge and the hope might not be realized. In other words, instead of, in the last resort, the industry being managed by experts, its policy might be settled for it as the result of promises made to the electorate by well-meaning, clever, but inexpert and misguided politicians.

On the other hand, the person responsible to Parliament for the policy pursued by those entrusted with the management of the industry would be, were he appointed as other Ministers are, liable to considerable political pressure. Of the two forms of political interference, however, this, in our humble opinion, could be overcome much the more easily.

CHAPTER VI

THE EXPORT TRADE

THE coal export trade presents to-day an extremely complex question which we approach with diffidence. Normally, though the detailed knowledge of the trade requires a lifetime fully to acquire, the underlying principles are simple. It is a mere matter of c.i.f.—cost, insurance and freight. If those three components of the total price are in favour of this country, this country gets the trade, if they are against, she loses the trade. Even in pre-war days, however, this simple business principle was being affected by the development in Germany of the view that for reasons other than purely economic reasons it is in certain circumstances desirable to capture foreign markets by selling at a loss. That is to say, the German rings such as the Westphalian Coal Syndicate were prepared to sell to the foreigner at a price below the total of c.i.f.

To-day the European international position is much more involved than in pre-war days. The French coalfields have been almost entirely destroyed. The Belgian coalfields have been seriously damaged. The Russian mines show under the Bolshevist regime a productivity so low as to be almost negligible. By Article 48 of the Treaty of Peace, France has been given " as compensation for the destruction of the coal mines in the North of France and as part payment towards the total reparation due from Germany for the damage resulting from the war " full and absolute possession of the important Saar Coalfield, and (Art. 50, Annex) all the deposits of coal situated within the Saar basin become the complete and absolute property of the French State.

By the Treaty Germany also loses Upper Silesia, which passes to Poland, who, however, undertakes (Art. 90) " to permit for a period of fifteen years the exportation to Germany of the products of the mines in any part of Upper Silesia transferred to Poland." Such exportation is to be free of export duties and on terms " necessary to secure that any such products shall be available for sale to purchasers in Germany on terms as favourable as are applicable to like products sold under similar conditions to purchasers in Poland or in any other country."

Germany further agrees (Art. 236, Annex v) to deliver seven million tons of coal per annum to France for ten years, and *in addition* " an amount of coal equal to the difference between the annual production before the war of the coal mines of the Nord and Pas de Calais, destroyed as a result of the war, and the production of the mines of the same area during the years in question : such delivery not to exceed twenty million tons in any one year of the first five years, and eight million tons in any one year of the succeeding five years."

Germany also undertakes to deliver to Belgium eight million tons of coal annually for ten years and to Italy the following quantities of coal :—

July, 1919 –	June, 1920	..	4,500,000	tons.
,, 1920 –	,, 1921	..	6,000,000	,,
,, 1921 –	,, 1922	..	7,500,000	,,
,, 1922 –	,, 1923	..	8,000,000	,,
,, 1923 –	,, 1924	..	8,500,000	,,

and the same annual amount of **8,500,000** up to the June of 1929. Luxemburg also has to receive an annual amount equal to the pre-war annual consumption of German coal in Luxemburg.[1]

The price to be paid for such deliveries are as follows :—

" (*a*) For overland delivery,[2] including delivery by barge, the German pithead price to German nationals, *plus* the freight to French, Belgian, Italian or Luxemburg frontiers, provided that the pithead price does not exceed the pithead price of British coal for export. In the case of Belgian bunker coal, the price shall not exceed the Dutch

---

[1] Since the above was written it is understood that in view of the shortage of coal in Germany and the miners' strike in Upper Silesia, the Allied and Associated Governments have had under consideration the reduction of the amounts which could be demanded under the terms of the Treaty of Peace.

[2] Art. 236, Annex. v, clause 6. At least two-thirds of the deliveries to Italy are required to be land borne.

bunker price. Railroad and barge tariffs should not be higher than the lowest similar rates paid in Germany.

(b) For sea delivery, the German export price f.o.b. (free on board) the German ports, or the British export price f.o.b. British ports, whichever may be the lower."

The result of the above in conjunction with the facts we have already given in previous chapters seems to be as follows :—

Granted a post-war productivity equal to that of the quinquennial period 1906–10 we have for the total output of all the coalfields which were German in 1914 the figure 145,918,000 tons.

Of this total Germany has lost by the cession of the Saar basin 14,412,000[1] tons annually and in addition she has to export for the next ten years to France, Italy and Belgium an annual average of 36,700,000 tons.

Thus, granted that Germany receives under the rights reserved to her the whole of the produce of the Upper Silesian mines, she has left for inland consumption and export other than compulsory export 145,918,000 minus 51,112,000 tons, or a total of 94,806,000 tons.

The above figure, however, is based on the very doubtful assumption that post-war productivity will equal that of the quinquennial period 1906–10.

---

[1] This figure is based on the output of the State mines in the Saar for 1910 (10,823,483) which was 75·10 per cent of the total output for the Saar coalfield.

At present we understand the German figures of output per man per shift are very low and average hardly more that 10 cwt., or rather less than half the pre-war man output for shift. This is doubtless a figure which will soon improve, but it is a matter of doubt how long it will take before the pre-war standard is reached. Again, in the summer of 1919 the German Socialisation Bill became law and it remains to be seen how the new organization will work. On the other hand, the 1914 output figures were in excess of those for the quinquennial period 1906–10. On the whole we incline to the view that Germany will not in the immediate future have a productivity rate as high as that estimated by us but that when she has recovered to some extent from the present adverse conditions, which are due to the war and are affecting her to a greater extent than this country, she will increase her productivity per man employed.

That she must make every effort to achieve such a result is obvious. In the spring of this year, and before the terms of the Peace Treaty had come into operation, Germany was suffering from a coal shortage. Thus, according to *Welthandel* for February 14th, 1919, " reports are arriving from the whole country of the closing down of individual establishments and in places of the entire local industries. Even in Upper Silesia the industries are crippled by the shortage of coal. In South Germany, East and West Prussia and Pomerania, which are furthest away from the coal districts, it is impossible to speak of industrial activity as existing to any extent worth mentioning." The *Kölnische Zeitung*, the *Weltwirtschaftszeitung* and the *Frankfurter Zeitung* tell the same tale.

It may be that such reports are false and were circulated to mislead. It is as yet too soon for us to be able to be certain of the industrial position in Germany; but it is probable that they correctly represent the present position. If we take the 1904 figures for German output and export we find that the output was 120,816,000 and the export 21,631,000.[1] This would leave for internal consumption in Germany 99,185,000 tons or roughly 4,000,000 tons more than will be available on our estimate. In considering these figures we must bear in mind the present low productivity per man and the fact that since 1904 Germany's internal demands have very considerably increased.

At the moment, of course, the position of Germany, as of other European countries, is admittedly serious. Mr. Hoover has stated officially that only two-thirds of the output necessary for European consumption is being obtained to-day in Europe.

To sum up it would appear that so far as Germany is concerned she will be a serious competitor with us for the French, Belgian and Italian markets but will probably not be in a position for many years seriously to compete with us in the

---

[1] See " Eight Hours," Committee Blue Book, Cd. 3506/7, Pt. 2, p. 282.

THE EXPORT TRADE 127

other markets and may actually have to become an importer herself.

We do not, however, see how in her present economic state it will be in any way possible for Germany to import this raw material. The foreign exchanges are so heavily against her and her need for other raw materials so great that we entirely agree with Sir Daniel Stevenson when he said: " It seems to me Germany must export a large quantity of coal to get in raw materials, and the sooner the better. I think that must be the policy of economists in Germany. They must export in order to get in raw material." As we have seen, however, under the terms of the Peace Treaty Germany will have to export on an average 36,700,000 tons a year or about 15,000,000 more tons than her entire export trade in 1904, and we doubt in view of the loss of the Saar and Upper Silesian fields whether she can possibly export any more.

We have dealt with the position of Germany at length because so far as the European market is concerned she has been, in the past, our most serious competitor. Apart from business with France, Belgium and Italy she would now appear to be eliminated *for the present*. In deciding upon the course to be taken by a country, however, it is desirable to take long views and there is but little doubt that if we rest upon our oars simply because our opponent has caught a crab we shall probably lose the race.

When we turn to consider our position with

reference to another most important competitor—America—a very different picture is presented. America's natural resources are greater than Britain's; her output per man is increasing and the British is decreasing; her getting-cost per ton is much lower than ours. Freights and tonnage alone enable us to hold our own, and so far as tonnage is concerned this country has suffered severely during the war while freights will soon decline from their present position.

From a paper prepared by the Engineers' Committee of the United States Fuel Administration entitled *Method of Fixing Prices of Bituminous Coal adopted by the United States Fuel Administration* it appears that in July, 1918, the general average price of 84 per cent of the output of bituminous coal in the United States was 2·162 $ per ton of 2000 lb. to which cost must be added 45 cents per ton to meet increased wage cost. This gives a total cost of 2·612 $ per 2000 lb. or reduced to English constants 12s. 3d. per ton. In arriving at this average the cheapest coals were calculated in with the dearer coals, but it is with the cheapest coals, i.e. those mined in West Virginia, that Great Britain would have to be prepared to compete, and the price of such coals is only 11s. per ton.

If we compare these figures with the average prices ruling for American bituminous coals in 1913[1] we find that the average for all bituminous

[1] See Part II, *Mineral Resources of the United States*, 1916, p. 910.

coals in that year was 1·18 $ per 2000 lb. and of West Virginia coal 1·01 $ per 2000 lb., these figures being slightly higher than those for any other year up to 1916 when prices rose to 1·32 $ and 1·18 $ per 2000 lb. respectively.

Converting into English constants we thus get 1913 prices of 5s. 6d. and 4s. 9d. per ton for all bituminous and for West Virginian respectively. We therefore have a rise in price from 1913–18 of from 6s. 9d. in the case of all bituminous and of 6s. 3d. in respect of West Virginian coal.

It is probable, however, that these 1918 prices could be cut and still leave the same margin between selling price and cost per ton as existed in 1913, for in the paper *Method of Fixing Prices, etc.*, above referred to 45·6 cents per 2000 lb.[1] was allowed as the average margin, whereas in an earlier paper issued in 1917 by the Chief Mining Engineer of the Bureau of Mines and entitled *Mining Costs and Selling Prices on Coal in the United States and Europe with Special Reference to Export Trade* the average margin allowed was only ·200 $ per 2000 lb. in 1913.[1] This would allow of the 1918 selling price being reduced by 1s. 1½d. without the 1913 margin being lowered.

It thus appears that the increase in the price of best Virginian coal up to September, 1918, was somewhere between 6s. 3d. and 5s. 0½d. per ton or say 5s. 7½d. per ton. In the same period British

---

[1] 45·6 cents per 2000 lb. = 2s. 1¼d. per ton ; ·200 $ per 2000 lb. = 11d. per ton.

coal increased by 13s. 7½d. per ton, leaving a difference of 8s. per ton in favour of America.

If we now compare the position as competitors of the two countries before the war and as regards the European market we shall see what lesson is to be derived from these figures.

If we take Italy as the importing country and Virginia coking coal and Durham coking coal respectively we get the following comparison for July, 1914.

West Virginia Coking Coal			Durham Coking Coal		
f.o.b. price	11	4	f.o.b. price	13	0
Freight	12	0	Freight	9	4
	23	4		22	4

The British thus obtained the market, the British price being 1s. less and the quality slightly better. But now, with the difference in f.o.b. price increased by 8s. against us, it would appear to follow that that market will go to America if the Italians find they can get it cheaper from America than from Germany even under the terms imposed by the Peace Treaty which compels Germany to supply at the lower of the two prices, German or British. If then the lower of these two prices is higher than the American, Italy will waive her option to purchase from Germany and the German will have so much more coal in hand to compete with us elsewhere. The same applies to France and

THE EXPORT TRADE 131

to Belgium except that as regards those two countries England is in a better position as regards freights.

If we now turn to the very important South Atlantic trade[1]—a trade which absorbed about seven million tons of our export tonnage in 1914—we find that the position there is also serious. In pre-war times, according to the evidence of Mr. Bowen, one of the greatest experts in this country on the subject, the British f.o.b. price was about 18s., and the American f.o.b. price 11s. or 12s. It was therefore necessary for the British to be in a position to save at least 6s. a ton on freight to get the trade. To-day, of course, freights both in the case of British and American ships have soared, but they will steady, and even if the pre-war levels are never reached there is no reason to believe that the *relative* levels will be decidedly affected in favour of Great Britain. We have therefore to keep our f.o.b. prices within 6s. of the American f.o.b. prices.

Now in the March of 1919, according to the particulars which Mr. Bowen presented to the Coal Industry Commission, America was in a position to offer a hundred thousand tons of the very best Pocahontas or New River coal at the price of 22s. 6d. per ton f.o.b. Newport News or Norfolk Va. To this figure must be added 10d. per ton for trimming.

---

[1] It should be observed that a coalfield has recently been proved in the Argentine.

To compete with this offer it would be necessary for the British Coal exporter, in the era when freights have levelled down, to be able to offer f.o.b. Cardiff first-class British steam coal at 29s. 4d. per ton. It is within the knowledge of everybody that if coal were exported at such a price to-day it would mean that the foreigner was obtaining it much more cheaply than the British manufacturer.

It must not be imagined that Great Britain has obtained her coal export trade in the past because the quality of her coal is superior to any other. With the exception of Welsh anthracite, which has no equal, the British coals, though of a very high standard, can be equalled by other countries. The trade was obtained because the price was right, as may be seen from the following f.o.b. prices for 1907 :[1]—

	s.	d.		
Newport Steam	15	6	f.o.b.	Newport.
Cardiff Steam	16	6	,,	Cardiff.
Westphalian	15	0	,,	Hamburg trimmed.
Westphalian	15	0	,,	Rotterdam ,,
Silesian	17	6	,,	Stettin
Russian	18	6	,,	Marinpol.
Pocahontas	13	5	,,	Norfolk Va.
Best Alabama	12	4½	,,	Pensacola.
Best Bengal	12	4½	,,	Calcutta.
Natal Navigation	17	0	f.a.s.	Durban.
Japanese	14	9	f.o.b.	Wakamatsu.
Japanese	17	0	,,	Nagasaki.

[1] " Eight Hours," Blue Book, Cd. 3506/7, Part II, p. 282.

THE EXPORT TRADE 133

England could thus in those days quote an f.o.b. price only some 2s. or 3s. in excess of the American f.o.b. price, with the result that the British c.i.f. to the South Atlantic was lower than the American.

Having now indicated in general outline the probable future of our coal export trade we will examine the extent of the problem which is thus presented to us.

The coal export figures for 1895, 1904 and 1913-1919 are as follows[1]:—

Period	Output	Inland Consumption and Bunkers	Export
1895	189,661,362	147,152,362	42,509,000
1904	232,816,000	167,375,000	65,441,000
1913	287,412,000	210,105,000	77,307,000
1914	265,643,000	203,185,000	32,456,000
1915	253,179,000	206,857,000	46,322,000
1916	255,846,000	213,917,000	41,929,000
1917	248,041,000	209,607,000	36,434,000
1918	226,557,000	195,937,000[2]	34,420,000
1919[3]	230,606,000	198,806,000	28,000,000

Since the above figures were compiled there has been a prolonged strike in our most important coalfield (Yorkshire) and it is probable, therefore,

[1] See "Eight Hours," Blue Book, Cd. 3506/7, Part II, p. 282; and Coal Industry Commission Blue Book, Appendix, Stage II, p. 56.
[2] Part came out of stocks in hand and 192,137,000 out of output.
[3] Estimate.

that the estimate for 1919 is optimistic. Ignoring this, however, as a chance occurrence that is not likely to enter into future calculations, we see that in order to obtain our pre-war position we need an export trade of some seventy million tons per annum.

We have already given figures as to price from which rosy conclusions can hardly be deduced, but even though the price could be brought down we shall still be confronted with the decline in output.

Now we believe that it is objectionable in considering output to take account of the decline which occurred in war-time. The conditions were absolutely abnormal. Four hundred thousand miners joined the forces. Development work was retarded. Untrained dilutees had to be brought into the mines. Many other and more technical difficulties arose preventing any record-breaking figures being reached or approached. Taking everything into account the industry acquitted itself well.

But, even though we dismiss from our minds the war-time reductions and the low output which will almost certainly appertain for some time, even though we look far into the future, it seems clear that with a reduced working day, which is expected by both the Government and the Miners to result in a reduction of 10 per cent in output, our available tonnage for export will not be as high as in 1914 until the number of our mines has sensibly increased. It is a matter for consideration whether any such increase is to be looked for while the sword of Damocles is hanging over the industry. Capital is hardly to be attracted to the speculation work of boring for coal and sinking shafts when the reward for success is a small guaranteed profit with the possibility of expropriation.

Even if we take the highest output ever reached, 287,412,000 for 1913, and reduce it by 10 per cent, we get only 258,671,000 tons. Clause v. of the Chairman's report indicates that 250,000,000 represents the more probable output, but even on the basis of 258,671,000 this leaves some 50,000,000 tons for export or a loss over 1913 of about 27,000,000 tons. If, on the other hand, we look at the immediate future we find only a small amount of coal available for export, even assuming that the irritating and trying restrictions on home consumption are maintained.

To sum up we see that once freights have levelled down, our coal cost per ton must be substantially reduced or one of two things must follow : (1) the British export trade will be lost to America or (2) the export trade must be in effect subsidized at the cost of the home consumer—the manufacturer—who will thus be heavily handicapped in his struggle for the world market. Even if the cost is brought down productivity must go up or there will be a very small margin of coal left for export.

Now it may occur to the reader that there is no

particular reason why any real sacrifices should be made to preserve this export trade. He may say, "Let it go, what does it matter?" It matters vitally and for the following among other reasons:—

Great Britain must import. This proposition may have required arguments to sustain it before the war, but now, with the memory of an unrestricted submarine campaign and its effect on our tables and our lives, it has become a self-evident fact.

Granted that Great Britain must import it follows that assuming the imports are not given to her she must pay for them. Two methods of payment exist—in money or in kind. Apart altogether from the question of exchange the volume of the import trade is such that payment in money is out of the question, it therefore follows that goods must be exported. *If she cannot get a market because of cost for her raw material coal she cannot get a market for her manufactured articles, the cost of which largely depends on the cost of coal.* She would have to get a market or starve, and consequently the price to the foreigner would have to come down below cost. To make up the loss the home consumer would have to pay more.[1]

[1] The first step in this necessary but very undesirable course was taken when, in calculating the increase of 6s. in the cost of coal to meet the Sankey increase and the reduction of hours, the export trade was excluded from the tonnage on which the increase could be placed. Already, therefore, the foreigner gets his coals relatively 6s. cheaper than the home consumer although actually he may be paying more.

The result would be that everything that is made would have to go up, as coal enters into the costing of every manufactured article. The further result would be that the cost of living would increase and that would result in further demands for higher wages. In these demands there is small reason to believe that the miners would not participate. As a consequence the cost of coal would go up again. The whole additional burden would have to fall on the home consumer and so on *ad infinitum,* or at least until it became evident that further rises could not take place. When that stage was reached the standard of life would have to come down and that would cause discontent and so on. The sequence of events is not favourable to us.

Again, bearing in mind the importance of our c.i.f. prices for any exported goods being lower than those of other countries with whom we are in competition, it follows that it is of the first importance for our freights to be low so that our f.o.b. prices can be high and the market still retained. This applies not only to coal but to every kind of export trade. One of the most satisfactory and effective ways of keeping freights low is to utilize carrying space fully *both ways.* Thus the freight on wheat from the Argentine to England will be lower if the ship bringing the cargo can go back to the Argentine with a good freight-paying cargo than if she has to go back in ballast. The result of such imports (and most of our imports are raw or semi-raw materials) coming in on ships the freight of which is low is that prices are low. But such freights are not low unless the ship takes back some article of value. We must therefore, for this purpose also, export.

But if we cannot, either because of lack or because of high cost, export our one raw material—coal—how are we to hope to find a market for our manufactured articles? And if we have no market for our manufactured articles how will it be possible to utilize ships both ways?

If a ship is not utilized both ways then the one way must be paid for at a rate high enough to enable the ship to earn on the one journey practically what she formerly earned both ways. This then would mean that freights will rise. If freights rise the f.o.b. price must come down if the c.i.f. is to remain at the same level. Again the sequence of events are not favourable.

There is yet another fact to be borne in mind, also pointing to the necessity of maintaining our coal export trade. The average gross profit per ton (of which a portion went to the Exchequer in relief of taxation) during the first three quarters of 1918 varied from 1s. 10·41d. to 3s. 10·41d. a ton. Of this profit by far the larger part was obtained from the export market. The table on the opposite page shows the position.

It thus appears clear that the home price would have been of necessity higher had the export trade not enabled the industry to make high profits in the war years. We have already seen that as soon as

	Quarter ending 31st March, 1918	Quarter ending 30th June, 1918	Quarter ending 30 Sept., 1918
Average receipts per ton of disposable coal.	19s. 10·49d.	20s. 5·65d.	25s. 1·32d.
Average cost per ton including royalties.	17s. 11d.	18s. 7·24d.	21s. 1·48d.
[1] Average profit per ton ..	1s. 11·49d.	1s. 10·41d.	3s. 10·41d.
Quantity of coal sold inland.	31,069,341 tons.	28,073,037 tons.	22,822,169 tons.
Average price per ton ..	18s. 7·24d.	18s. 9·1d.	22s. 8·05d.
Profit per ton	8·24d.	1·86d.	1s. 6·57d.
Quantity of coal sold for export.	9,217,210 tons.	9,911,600 tons.	9,750,214 tons.
Average price per ton ..	24s. 5·8d.	25s. 7·59d.	31s. 1·86d.
Profit per ton	6s. 6·8d.	7s. 0·35d.	10s. 0·38d.

[1] "The average profit per ton" includes miscellaneous receipts not arising from the sale of coal to the following extent:—

  March .. .. .. 3.16d. per ton.
  June .. .. .. 3.65d. ,,
  September .. .. 3.62d. ,,

the world market and world freights return to the normal such high profits will not, in all probability, be maintainable. The high prices charged the neutrals during the war years will be unobtainable, and it appears to follow, as a matter of course, that with export trade profits down home trade profits must go up or the total profits earned by the industry be reduced.

That the industry could stand a reduction of the profits made in 1918 is probable, but it must be borne in mind that since that date wages have substantially increased and the hours of work have been substantially reduced, and, although the financial stability of the industry has been to some extent protected by the increase of the price of coal to the home consumer, this has only enabled profits to be made on the basis of an average of 1s. 2d. a ton.

If therefore, *at present*, while good profits are obtainable in the coal export trade, that trade is lost, there must be a reaction on the home market in the direction of a further increase in price to make possible the earning of even the limited average profit of 1s. 2d. a ton—an average figure which cannot be regarded as unduly high for a speculative industry involving heavy capital outlays and the risk of serious losses. On the other hand, when it becomes necessary to cut export prices in order to obtain export business it is manifest that on the basis of the present cost of production the export profits will tend to dis-

THE EXPORT TRADE 141

appear and this again will react unfavourably upon the home market while the elimination of the export trade as an unprofitable concern will, as we have seen, have such disastrous effects upon our national finances, and will threaten us with such dangers due to the impossibility of importing indefinitely without exporting, that we shall be compelled to trade even at a loss—a condition of affairs which will reflect still more seriously upon the home market.

Much more could be added, but it appears that already enough has been said to make it obvious that it is necessary for the production of coal to go up and for the price of coal f.o.b. to come down. The second of these necessities is dependent upon the first, for it is not practical politics to diminish wages. The whole problem thus reduces itself to a question of the modes and methods whereby production can be increased.

CHAPTER VII

THE HOME CONSUMER

WE have now examined, in a very slight and imperfect manner, the export market, and we have seen that unless this country is to be heavily handicapped as regards its internal industries, and unless the cost of living is still further to rise, it is imperative that our coal export shall increase, and for this to be possible output must go up and price must come down. We will now turn and consider the position of the home consumer.

So far as mere inconvenience is concerned any shortage of coal is most directly experienced in the home. The supplies of household fuel, gas, electricity, all have to be reduced either because the amount which may be supplied is limited or because the cost is so high that economy is necessary.

To-day in Great Britain both causes operate with the result that considerable personal inconvenience and discomfort is experienced. This in itself is very undesirable.

While any serious shortage of supplies exist,

THE HOME CONSUMER 143

however, one is confronted by a choice of evils. Either the home or the factory must go short if any portion of the reduced output is to be available for export. Nor is it solely a matter of saving coal that the Household Fuel and Lighting Orders aimed at. Had economy in use been the sole aim it is doubtful whether the policy could have been justified as a comparatively small saving was effected at a very considerable cost both of money and of convenience. It was, however, rather in the fact that rationing protects the man with the shallow purse against the man with the big bank balance that we have to look for the real justification of these Orders. With an admitted shortage, a greater demand than supply, a rising price, the wealthy could, and experience in other matters shows that in many cases they would, have bought and stocked. The result would have been that the poor would have had to go without.

It must, however, be conceded that even though the Household Fuel and Lighting Orders are fully justified and absolutely necessary, they are still irritating and vexatious. We all look forward to the time when these and other interferences with our liberty of action will be swept away. But they cannot be swept away lest worse evils take their place, unless and until the enemy they were intended to defeat has been defeated. That enemy was not Germany but Inadequate Production.

We must therefore be prepared to expect for

some time to come a rationing of our household supply of coal, gas and electricity. Even, however, were the rationing lifted we should still find it necessary to economize strictly owing to the great increase in price.

The increase in the cost of coal has been steadily rising for many years. When the first Durham sliding scale for the regulation of the wages of hewers and underground workers was fixed in 1877 the following was the scale fixed :—

First Durham Scale of 1877

Price (in shillings)		Wage (in percentages)
At and above	But below	
5·4	5·4	7½ % Reduction
5·8	5·8	5 % ,,
		Present Rate
6·4	6·4	5 % Advance
7·0	7·0	10 % ,,
7·8	7·8	15 % ,,
8·4	8·4	20 % ,,
9·0	9·0	25 % ,,
9·8	9·8	30 % ,,
10·4	10·4	35 % ,,
10·4	11·0	40 % ,,
11·8	11·8	45 % ,,
12·4	12·4	50 % ,,
13·0	13·0	55 % ,,
13·8 and so on	13·8	60 % ,,

From the above it will be seen that in 1877 the Durham pit-head price was between 5s. 8d. and 6s. 4d. per ton. We have, indeed, seen a coal invoice of the early eighties in which coal was charged at 4s. 6d. per ton delivered. By 1914 the pit-head price for best Derby (household) coal had risen to something in the neighbourhood of 11s. 6d.; by 1918 this figure had jumped to 23s. 3d., and by the autumn of 1919 had increased to 32s. 0d.[1]

According to the figures put in by Mr. Errington Brewis, when giving evidence before the Coal Industry Commission,[2] given the above pit-head prices, the average selling price of 35s. 6d. and 43s. 6d. for 1914 and 1918 respectively allowed the coal merchant to retain a profit of 10¾d. per ton in 1914, and 1s. 8d. a ton in 1918. In view of the lessened value of money these two sums are practically equivalent.

---

[1] In 1915 a Departmental Committee of the Board of Trade sat to consider the "causes of the present rise in the retail price of coal sold for domestic use." Its Report, issued on the 24th March, 1915, is to be obtained from any bookseller (Cd. 7866/15). In the course of that Report the Committee state (paragraph 8): "We have to report that, in our opinion, the initial cause of the increase of recent price, ranging from 7s. to 11s. per ton, above the winter prices of 1913–14, was a deficiency of supply as compared with demand; and in particular a deficiency of supply in London. . . . The apprehension of a coal famine caused orders to pour in from consumers who had any storage accommodation." The Committee further state (paragraph 32): "We have seen that a slight deficiency may create a situation which is a hardship to the consumer and a danger to industry, and we are of the opinion that, in the absence of any regulating measures, these hardships and dangers are likely to be indefinitely increased."

[2] Coal Industry Commission Blue Book, Vol. 3, Appendix 46 Stage I).

Even this serious increase in selling price would undoubtedly have been higher had it not been for the fact that the railway rate remained constant with the result that the railways do not pay.

For the detailed account of the various small items that go to form the total cost of transport from pit-head to consumer, the reader is referred to the Coal Industry Commission Blue Book, but we will indicate the chief items and the extent of the rise in each case :—

The wages of loaders in 1914 came to 9d. a ton, with war bonus these wages in 1918 amounted to 1s. 6d. The carmen absorbed, with driving money, $10\frac{1}{2}$d. of the total in 1914, now their share is 1s. 10d. The wages of trolleymen have gone up from £2 2s. 7d. to £5 1s. 6d. ; the carmen who got £1 11s. 5d. now receive £3 4s. 10d. ; the loaders to-day get £3 12s. 8d. instead of the weekly pre-war wage of £1 16s. 8d. The cost of bags, of horses, of feeding stuffs have enormously increased, so that such items which used to account for $11\frac{1}{4}$d. now amount to 2s. 6d. Establishment charges which once were 1s. $1\frac{1}{2}$d. have now risen to 3s. 6d., an increase which it is difficult to accept as necessary, as it is notorious that management and clerical salaries have not risen to the same extent as those of manual workers, while the above increase would suggest that they have increased to a greater extent.

According to the above it will be seen that, granted a pit-head price of 23s. 6d., railway rate of

6s. 4d. and waggon hire of 1s. 6d., total 31s. 1d., the cost to the household consumer is 43s. 6d. in order for the middleman to earn a profit of 1s. 8d. This gives for distribution a cost from station to home of 10s. 9d. On the other hand, the Co-operative Societies gave evidence to the effect that such cost varied according as the district was difficult: medium, or convenient, from 8s. 5d. to 7s. 6d. and 5s. 8d. Even granted that a small saving could be effected here, or granted that the pit-head price has increased greatly since 1870, we have still no explanation of how it was possible to sell coal at 4s. 6d. delivered in those days while to-day the railway rate alone to the district where that coal was delivered is in excess of the total price then.

The fact, of course, is that the value of money has depreciated greatly since 1870 and, at the same time, those cheap means of transit—the canals and the roads—have been neglected. The time has come when, for such goods as coal, it is of the first importance that cheap means of transport shall be developed. It is in our opinion absurd that as much as 13s. a ton should have to be paid for railway transit alone in England when the freight from America to Naples in 1914 was only 12s. We believe that a substantial reduction in price could be effected by a cheaper system of transit for such articles as coal which do not quickly deteriorate and the speedy delivery of which is not essential. We cannot believe that any sound reason exists for paying 14s. 10½d.[1] for transport to the port of Penzance when the freight from Durham to Naples was, in 1914, 9s. 4d. These, however, are matters not connected with the Coal Industry so much as with the transport systems of this country; they are therefore not points for us to pursue.

When we consider the reason for the high present-day pit-head price we find that the position is as follows :—

Taking the quarter ended 30th September, 1918, there were raised in Great Britain :

54,592,000 tons of coal.

Of this total production there were consumed at the collieries or given away to the colliery employees :

3,498,132 tons of coal,

so that there was available for sale :

51,093,868 tons of coal.

The average pit-head price was 24s. 9·99d.

Of this price the following items absorbed the amount shown :—

	s.	d.
Wages	13	7·56
Stores and timber	3	6·48
Other costs	1	4·30
Profits	4	6·98
Royalties		7·14
Total	23	8·46

[1] See Coal Industry Commission Blue Book, Stage I, Appendix 48.

THE HOME CONSUMER 149

These figures speak for themselves and do not call for explanation. The extraordinary cost of stores and timber is mainly accounted for by the cost of timber, which jumped up from between 1d. and 6d. per ton of coal raised, according to the district, to between 1s. and 2s., due mainly to the fact that it was necessary to rely on home-grown supplies instead of on imported timber, with the result that for the inferior home-grown article the consumer had to pay an enormously enhanced price.

The wage item of 13s. 7·56d. has, since the above figures were compiled, been substantially increased by the increase granted by the " Sankey " Report of the 20th March, 1919. This increase of 2s. a day for all colliery workers, in conjunction with the reduction in the hours of labour and the increase in piece-work rates necessary to carry out the Government's pledge that the piece-workers' earnings will not be reduced in consequence of the reduction in hours, has necessitated a further increase of 6s. a ton in the cost of coal.

This increase is arrived at as follows :[1]—

Estimated deficiency on the working of the coal industry for a period of 12 months from 16th July, 1919 .. £46,600,000

Estimated output of coal for 12 months from 16th July, 1919 .. .. Tons 217,000,000

[1] See Statement presented to Parliament, Cmd. 252/19.

Less quantity upon which an increased price would not be effective, viz. :—	Tons	Tons
Coal for consumption at collieries, estimated at ..	18,000,000	
Coal supplied for miners' use based on the quantity supplied in 1918, viz. 5,850,000 tons, say ..	6,000,000	
Coal for exports and bunkers sold at open market prices above the minimum	32,000,000	
		56,000,000
Quantity of coal over which the estimated deficiency of £46,600,000 is spread		161,000,000

$$\text{Increase in price of coal} = \frac{£46,600,000}{161,000,000 \text{ tons}} = 5s.\ 9\tfrac{1}{2}d., \text{ say } 6s.$$

The difference between this estimate of the increase necessary and the estimate of 4s. 6d. per ton contained in Table VI of the schedules presented by the Controller of Coal Mines to the Coal Industry Commission is due mainly to the fact that in arriving at the estimate of 4s. 6d. no deduction had been made in arriving at the amount of coal on which the charge could be placed, either for the amount of coal which the collieries themselves consumed, or for the amount supplied for miners' use, or for the amounts for export and bunkers.

The increase in the cost of household fuel affects

THE HOME CONSUMER 151

our comfort, the increase of the cost of coal to manufacturers causes an advance in the cost of living all round and renders us less able to hold our own in the world's markets. From the purely economic point of view the effect in the trade of the country due to the extra charge paid by the manufacturer is much more important than that due to the increased cost of household or gas coal.

It is a truism that coal enters into the costing of every manufactured article, but it may be of service to the reader if, instead of laying down vague generalities, we give the figures showing the probable increase which occur for every 1s. which is added to the cost of coal.

If we accept, as we are entitled to, the conclusions arrived at as a result of questions put to their members by the Federation of British Industries, we find that 1s. on the cost of coal means a 5 per cent increase on January, 1919, fuel cost and the following increases in the following materials :—

Electricity and gas	$2\frac{1}{2}$ %
Steel	4s. per ton
Copper	5s. per ton
Brass	5s. per ton
Building material (bricks, etc.)	1·25 %
Machinery	$2\frac{1}{2}$ %
Freight	1·25 %
Wool and worsted	·50 %
Dyeing	·20 %
Hosiery	·25 %
Flour	1d. per sack
Brewing	$2\frac{1}{2}$ %
Heavy chemicals	$2\frac{1}{2}$ %

Each of the above tend to react one upon the other with the result that the gross increase in cost is considerably higher in the case of any particular article than that increase which is due directly to fuel cost. Thus, for example, in silk-weaving not only has an increase in price to be charged to make up the increased fuel cost of driving the machinery, but the new machinery, new buildings, etc., that may be required cost more, and so on. As a result for silk we find that 1s. a ton on coal means a direct increase of ·3 per cent, but a direct and indirect increase of ·54 per cent. Again, in the case of rivets, bolts and nuts the direct increased cost is estimated at ·625 per cent, but the direct and indirect increase at 2·5 per cent.

The above figures are based on returns made to a Federation who were concerned to show that any increase in the cost of coal would have a prejudicial effect upon industry. They are therefore not impartial and are not as valuable as official returns. To that extent they may be discounted, but they cannot be entirely ignored.

We can, perhaps, adequately check them by showing the consumption of coal per ton of steel and by seeing how such consumption agrees with the above estimated increase in the cost of steel by 4s. a ton of steel for every 1s. on the ton of coal.

If reference is made to Stage I, Appendix 52 of the Coal Industry Commission Blue Book, it will be found that Mr. Wallace Thorneycroft, one of the greatest experts in this country on the question of steel production and one well known in the coal industry also, commits himself to the following figures as the result of returns made by a number of representative iron and steel manufacturers :—

CONSUMPTION OF COAL PER TON OF PIG-IRON

	1912	1913	1914	1915	1916
Coal consumed per ton of pig-iron produced	Cwt. 38·08	Cwt. 38·21	Cwt. 39·04	Cwt. 39·46	Cwt. 40·08

CONSUMPTION OF PIG-IRON PER TON OF STEEL (COLD METAL PROCESS)

	1912	1913	1914	1915	1916
Pig-iron consumed per ton of finished and semi-finished steel ..	Cwt. 17·50	Cwt. 17·40	Cwt. 18·27	Cwt. 18·98	Cwt. 17·84

CONSUMPTION OF PIG-IRON PER TON OF STEEL (MOLTEN METAL PROCESS)

	1912	1913	1914	1915	1916
Pig-iron consumed per ton of finished and semi-finished steel ..	Cwt. 19·14	Cwt. 19·19	Cwt. 18·53	Cwt. 18·06	Cwt. 17·31

Consumption of Coal per Ton of Ingot Moulds

	1912	1913	1914	1915	1916
Consumption of coal per ton of ingot moulds	Cwt. 7·64	Cwt. 7·13	Cwt. 7·02	Cwt. 7·87	Cwt. 8·33

Consumption of Ingot Moulds per Ton of Finished and Semi-finished Steel

	1912	1913	1914	1915	1916
Consumption of ingot moulds per ton of finished and semi-finished steel	Cwt. ·58	Cwt. ·57	Cwt. ·60	Cwt. ·66	Cwt. ·69

Consumption of Coal per Ton of Ferro-Manganese

	1912	1913	1914	1915	1916
Consumption of coal per ton of ferro-manganese	Cwt. 68·08	Cwt. 72·61	Cwt. 65·48	Cwt. 66·07	Cwt. 65·11

Consumption of Ferro-Manganese per Ton of Finished and Semi-finished Steel

	1912	1913	1914	1915	1916
Consumption of ferro-manganese per ton of finished and semi-finished steel	Cwt. ·33	Cwt. ·32	Cwt. ·35	Cwt. ·35	Cwt. ·37

THE HOME CONSUMER 155

Consumption of Coal used in all Processes from the Point at which the Pig-iron is Delivered at the Steel Works
(Cold Metal Process)

	1912	1913	1914	1915	1916
Consumption	Cwt. 40·60	Cwt. 41·32	Cwt. 46·82	Cwt. 45·97	Cwt. 42·86

Consumption of Coal used in all Processes from the Point at which the Pig-iron is Delivered at the Steel Works
(Molten Metal Process)

	1912	1913	1914	1915	1916
Consumption	Cwt. 17·79	Cwt. 17·92	Cwt. 17·69	Cwt. 18·77	Cwt. 18·64

From the above it will be found that for the cold metal process it requires 81·55 tons of coal to make one ton of steel. If to this is added 3·70 cwt. of coal necessary to raise and transport ores we get a grand total of 85·25 cwt. With the molten metal process, allowing the same amount for raising and transporting coal, we get 59·97 cwt. of coal necessary to produce one ton of steel.

If we take the entire steel output of the kingdom we find that about three-quarters of the whole is produced by the cold metal process and about one-quarter by the molten metal process.

We thus get

$$\frac{3 \times 85{\cdot}25 + 59{\cdot}97}{4} = 78{\cdot}93 \text{ cwt.}$$

as the average amount of coal used per ton of steel, and to this must be added a figure to cover the consumption of fuel by the tin-plate makers and re-rollers, so that the Federation's calculation of 80 cwt. appears to be substantially correct.

We thus see that an increase of 6s. in a ton of coal results in the following among other increases :

Article	£	s.	d.	Quantity
Steel	1	4	0	ton
Copper	1	10	0	,,
Brass	1	10	0	,,
Flour	0	0	6	sack
Beer		15 %		
Wool		3 %		
Machinery		15 %		

The above increases, however, are calculated on the basis of direct cost and on the assumption that the increase is spread over the whole industry. As we have seen, the actual cost direct and indirect may be much more. It is also to be borne in mind that it may be found impossible to charge these prices to the foreigner as, by so doing, we might lose our export trade. If this should be so it follows that the whole burden would fall on the home market, when we should again find ourselves

THE HOME CONSUMER 157

involved in that unfortunate sequence which we described in the previous chapter. Again the outlook is not favourable to us.

What then are we to do ? Every one desires that the miner's standard of living shall be as high as it possibly can be consonant with the industrial prosperity of this country. At present we are of the opinion that it is not too high, and that owing to the depreciation of the currency or, in other words, the increased cost of living, that it is not substantially higher than in pre-war days. It is not therefore, in our opinion, desirable to attack the problem by seeking to reduce wages quite apart from the fact that any such attempt would undoubtedly be resisted.

We repeat, What then are we to do ? The only hope, so far as we know, lies in increased production. A sensible increase *in productivity per man* would greatly ease the situation. An annual increase due to employing more men would help us with our export but to nothing like the same extent, for the wage ratio would still be so high that we should have difficulty in obtaining the market, but if the men realize, as we believe they will, that the whole prosperity of the community depends on them giving value for money, on their working their best during the shortened hours which now apply, if the management, despite present uncertainties, doubts and difficulties, decide to abandon *laissez-faire* and, for the credit of their profession and the good of the country, exercise their undoubted ability to increase by every means in their power the output of coal, if, and this is the most important if of all, the men and the masters look upon each other as decent members of the same commonwealth, whose interests are not hopelessly diverse, and decide to work side by side in amity until at least reason and argument rather than passion and prejudice shall have decided whether the present system of capital and labour shall continue or disappear, then we believe this country will secure its hard-won peace and will retain its proud eminence among the people of the world.

We adventure one other suggestion for what it is worth, knowing that it is directed to a class of men, many of the most eminent of which we have met and for whom we entertain the highest respect —the Trade Union leaders. We suggest that the time is soon coming, if it is not already arrived, when Trade Unions will have to pursue other aims than the mere improvement of conditions of labour. The time is coming when wages will be as high as they can go and when hours will be as reduced as they can be conformably to a prosperous industry, without which all the rest is useless. It will therefore be necessary for the Trade Unions to find fresh channels of activity if they are not to find themselves the prey of disloyal followers who, ignorant of great policies, seek momentary glory in the pursuit of impossible claims. Every responsible Trade Union leader knows how grievous a blow

THE HOME CONSUMER 159

such ill-considered action causes the industry, the Unions and, through them, the workers.

We therefore ask all those, and there are many, among the Trade Union leaders who desire to throw their weight on the side of industrial peace to cast their minds back into last century and consider what mighty strides in *managerial* efficiency followed from the elevation of management into a skilled profession, and we ask them to consider whether it is not possible for them to lead a movement having for its object the increased efficiency of the worker by the elevation of the worker into a manual profession in which the skilled man should be able to rank above the slacker and the bad workman, an elevation of status based not on money but upon merit, efficiency, ability.

It is doubtful, however, whether even though the worker and the management respectively increase in efficiency, it will be possible for some time to come to increase production to the necessary extent. The 250,000,000 tons indicated in the Chairman's second report will only very inadequately meet our present needs and it is consequently desirable to see whether those needs cannot be reduced without adversely affecting industry.

If we turn to the Final Report of the Coal Conservation Committee[1] which sat in 1917 to consider this matter, we shall find that the coal

[1] Cd. 9084/18.

consumption involved in the production of motive power in this country was at that date 80,000,000 tons, equal in value at present pit-head price to not less than £100,000,000.

During the last twenty-five years the coal consumption per horse-power throughout the country has been halved, but in spite of this the total amount used has increased. This proves that the demand for power becomes greater and greater. There is no reason to believe that this tendency will alter, especially when we bear in mind the fact that in the United States the amount of power used per worker was already, in 1917, 56 per cent more than in this country owing to the larger use of machinery in the States than in Great Britain.

In the words of the Committee: " The best cure for low wages is more motive power. Thus the solution of the workman's problem, and also that of his employer, is the same, viz. the greatest possible use of power." We are thus faced with the need for more power with a declining coal output, or if not a declining coal output at least with an output which cannot be expected largely to increase in the near future.

It thus becomes of the first moment to see that the coal that is produced is converted into terms of power in the best and most economical manner possible, and it has been demonstrated by the experience of the last decade that the most economical means of applying power to industry is the electric motor.

THE HOME CONSUMER 161

Further, to-day our railway systems are overloaded; our rail transport is expensive. Were the coal converted into power at or near the colliery districts and conveyed in the form of electricity from super-power stations enormous savings in work and cost would be effected. Beyond and above this saving would be that accruing from the most economical use of the coal, for in great generating plants it would be economically possible to utilize to the utmost the vast number of by-products obtainable from coal when properly consumed. Poor coal, which to-day it does not pay to raise and which is thrown into the gob and lost, could be utilized and made to do its share of the nation's work. Coal tars, oils, dyes, fertilizers and the hundred and one valuable products obtainable from the distillation of coal could be obtained on a properly large scale from the coal before it was consumed in the boiler, furnace or producer. The cost of electricity could be immensely reduced and our homes made brighter and more comfortable without any increase in our working expenses.

In the words of the Committee: " If such a system were inaugurated it may be confidently stated that on the basis of the extent to which power is used at present a saving of 55,000,000 tons of coal per annum can be expected. Taking the value of this coal for export purposes as 10s. per ton,[1] the national advantage of the charge,

[1] This figure of 10s. per ton is stated to be lower than the 1917 figure. It is of course much less than the present-day figure as we have seen.

available for interest on capital, is, say, £27,500,000 in coal alone. Alternatively, if this 55,000,000 tons of coal were used for extended and new industrial processes, some 15,000,000 horse-power continuously throughout the year would be available for the purpose.

" This saving of £27,500,000 per annum takes no account of the following additional and important advantages which would directly result from the establishment of an efficient electric power supply system throughout the country :—

1. A reduction in the cost of transport in carrying coal.

2. A possible saving in coal consumption for domestic purposes.

3. The reduction in the cost of coal handling involved in house-to-house delivery and general coal distribution.

4. The great advantages and economies which would result from the more extended use of electricity in the household for heating, cooking and cleaning purposes in the way of labour-saving devices, reduction of smoke, increased cleanliness, etc.

5. The possibility of utilizing the coal at present left in the pits or otherwise wasted.

6. The possibility of extracting by-products, etc., before consuming the coal for power purposes.

7. The increase in railway electrification, with its attendant advantages."

In the opinion of the Committee all these

savings and advantages, even were coal valued at a pit-head price of 10s. a ton, can hardly be put at less than £100,000,000 per annum.

To obtain these great advantages recommendations were made by the Committee in April, 1917. Following upon that the matter was considered by the Electric Power Supply Committee[1] appointed by the Board of Trade who in turn made concrete proposals in April, 1918. These various recommendations were favourably considered by the Government and action along the lines indicated was decided upon. In time an Electricity Bill was drafted and is before us.

It is a matter for some concern that this vital question of a cheap and abundant supply of electricity should not have been more actively pursued. The difficulties in the way of the reformer are undoubtedly great. Jealousies exist, vested interests have to be overcome, but the need is urgent and will soon be critical.

[1] Report, Cd. 9062/18.

CHAPTER VIII

WAGES AND DISPUTES

TO obtain for the workers a reasonable standard of life has for many years been the aim of all Trade Unions, and it is consequently not a matter for surprise that wage questions should have been the main cause of labour disputes which, despite the very elaborate machinery which has been devised to prevent such disputes developing into strikes, often, indeed too often, result in stoppages of work.

In the coal-mining industry the mode adopted for the regulation of the earnings of the persons employed is complicated, not merely by the fact that much of the work is piece-work varying with natural conditions, but also by the further facts that there has been in operation now for many years a sliding scale arrangement varying district by district, and that since 1912 the Coal Mines (Minimum Wage) Act of that year has provided for the payment of a minimum day wage to all underground workers.

In all such matters the industry is organized into districts, and consequently it is only possible, when describing the wage situation generally, to

WAGES AND DISPUTES

state the position approximately, for what may be true for the majority of districts would not be accurate as regards the minority. Generally, however, the position as regards wages may be stated as follows :—

Toward the end of the seventies or in the early years of the eighties of last century the various day wage rates and piece-work items (cutting prices, etc.) were placed upon a standard basis, district by district, and colliery by colliery in each district.

The differences in rates and prices thus fixed for even separate collieries in the same coalfield or district for the same work, were due to the fact that owing to natural conditions and differences in the economic value of the coal produced, higher standards could be paid in one colliery than in another.

The resulting standards are known as the 1877, 1879, or 1880 standards, as the case may be. The percentage of wages payable on these standards rose or fell according to the ascertained nett selling price of coal[1] in a particular district. This automatic arrangement lasted until the sliding scale was abolished and replaced, in the nineties and the early years of the present century, by Conciliation Board agreements.

Under the Conciliation Board agreements selling price was only one factor in the determination of what wage should be paid during the quarter under review. The wage now fluctuated not only with the selling price of coal but also with certain other

[1] In Shropshire the sliding scale formerly followed the selling price of iron and not of coal.

factors such as the volume of trade and the profits of the owners. Such profits were not, however, disclosed to the men who were consequently unable to ascertain with precision whether this variant had been taken fully into account. The fluctuations which occurred, both under the sliding scale arrangements and the Conciliation Board agreements, were considerable, and a graph showing the variations contains many peaks and valleys, for reductions as well as increases frequently occurred.

In the year 1915 the old standard was in many districts replaced by a new standard known as the 1915 standard. By that year, owing to the operation of the sliding scale arrangements and the Conciliation Board agreements, the percentage payable on the old standard rates had increased very sensibly. Thus, in the case of the Federated Area, it had increased by 85 per cent, so that the piece rate or the day rate for any class of work or grade of labour was 85 per cent higher in 1915 than it was when the old standard was fixed.

In such a case, i.e. when the increase was 85 per cent, the new standard was arrived at by adding 50 per cent to the old standard. If this new standard be called x the new rate in the case given (i.e. where the rate was 85 per cent higher than when the old standard was fixed) would be $x+(23\frac{1}{3}$ per cent of $x)$. This new standard again fluctuated according to the Conciliation Board agreements, even as the old standard had varied. By 1917 it had increased by about 56 per cent.

WAGES AND DISPUTES 167

In 1916, to meet the increased cost of living, a War Bonus was agreed to between the owners and the men. This War Bonus must be sharply distinguished from the War Wage which was subsequently granted by the Controller of Coal Mines to meet the increased cost of living due to the war. The War Bonus was also given to meet the increased cost of living, but it was calculated in an entirely different way from the War Wage.

The War Bonus was fixed in many districts at 18 per cent of the 1915 rate. That is to say, in the case given, it would be: 18 per cent of the 1915 standard plus $23\frac{1}{3}$ per cent. It thus varied man by man according to the man's earnings. It was also a wage, and consequently was not payable unless the man had earned wages.

In 1917, and again in 1918, a War Wage of 1s. 6d. per day (or, in the case of persons under sixteen years of age, 9d. per day) was granted, the total War Wage after the second grant was made being 3s. and 1s. 6d. per day respectively. This was an increase of a flat rate nature given equally to all persons in the industry and not affecting in any way the Conciliation Board percentage increases. The two arrangements ran side by side and proceeded on entirely different principles.

The War Wage was in many ways not a wage at all. It was not chargeable to the employer but came out of a special fund formed by a 4s. increase per ton on the selling price of coal. It was payable to any person " able and willing to work," whether he in fact worked or not, except that if the cause which prevented him from working was a strike, he did not get War Wage though himself willing to work. It has been the cause of a great number of disputes and of some strikes. There can be little doubt that this War Wage scheme is open to many serious objections, but it has the advantage of keeping a bonus based on a temporary depreciation of currency distinct from ordinary wages, and it gives to all the same increase—a fairer arrangement than that which gives more to one man than to another when the cause of the rise is not the reward of merit but increase of the price of necessities which all must purchase, and which affect all equally or nearly equally.

The flat-rate principle was also, of course, adopted by the signatories to the Interim Report of the Coal Industry Commission which was accepted by the Government. Under the recommendations of that Report every colliery worker received 2s. a day increase whether day-wage men or piece-workers. Further, when the reduction in hours took place on the 16th July last, a piece-work adjustment was made, designed to enable a piece-worker to earn in the new hours as much as he had earned in the old. No such adjustment was found necessary when the Eight Hours Act was passed. Although it would seem that on this point at least the miners were treated with eminent justness, if not indeed with generosity, it was as a result of a slight divergence of opinion as to the method of calculating the adjustment that the Yorkshire strike of 1919 took place, without any attempt being made to negotiate the matter with the party against whom the strike was directed. Such ill-considered action is, however, extremely rare.

From what we have already said it will be seen that the wages earned by persons employed in the coal-mining industry rise and fall according as certain variants, such as the cost of coal, rise and fall, except that in the case of the War Wage and the so-called Sankey Increase, a flat-rate advance was given. It happens somewhat frequently, however, that the men in a particular stall, or mine district, or colliery, or coalfield are not satisfied with the rate of pay arrived at by taking the basis plus percentages, and in such cases all the material is present for a local upheaval which may result in a strike which has a tendency to spread. To meet such cases very complete negotiating machinery exists, which we shall describe hereafter.

It should be understood, however, that a considerable proportion of the workers are piece-workers, whose rates of pay are on the tonnage system, the tonnage got per man being ascertained by owner's weigher and checked by the check-weigher (appointed and paid by the coal getters) who knows the stall from which each tub of coal comes by the signs which are chalked on the coal before it leaves the stall. Generally speaking it may be stated that the majority of hewers, getters, putters and trammers are piece-workers. Some-

has in fact worked or not, except that if the cause which prevented him from working was a strike, he did not get War Wage though himself willing to work. It has been the cause of a great number of disputes and of some strikes. There can be little doubt that this War Wage scheme is open to many serious objections, but it has the advantage of keeping a bonus based on a temporary depreciation of currency distinct from ordinary wages, and it gives to all the same increase—a fairer arrangement than that which gives more to one man than to another when the cause of the rise is not the reward of merit but increase of the price of necessities which all must purchase, and which affect all equally or nearly equally.

The flat-rate principle was also, of course, adopted by the signatories to the Interim Report of the Coal Industry Commission which was accepted by the Government. Under the recommendations of that Report every colliery worker received 2s. a day increase whether day-wage men or piece-workers. Further, when the reduction in hours took place on the 16th July last, a piece-work adjustment was made, designed to enable a piece-worker to earn in the new hours as much as he had earned in the old. No such adjustment was fo...
necessary when the Eight Hours Act was
Although it would seem that
the miners were treated w
no indeed with generosi'
slight divergence of o

WAGES AND DISPUTES

calculating the adjustment that the Yorkshire strike of 1919 took place, without any attempt being made to negotiate the matter with the party against whom the strike was directed. Such ill-considered action is, however, extremely rare.

From what we have already said it will be seen that the wages earned by persons employed in the coal-mining industry rise and fall according to certain variants, such as the cost of coal, rise and fall, except that in the case of the War Wage and the so-called Sankey Increase, a flat-rate advance was given. It happens somewhat frequently, however, that the men in a particular stall, or mine district, or colliery, or coalfield are not satisfied with the rate of pay arrived at by taking the basis plus percentages, and in such cases all the material is present for a local upheaval which may result in a strike which has a tendency to spread. To meet such cases very complete negotiating machinery exists, which we shall describe hereafter.

It should be understood, however, that a considerable proportion of the workers are not

times the piece rate is not capable of being fixed on a tonnage basis, as, for instance, in the case of stonemen, but is calculated by area.

The fixing of price-lists, as the piece-workers' lists of rates are called, is a very intricate matter which calls for expert knowledge of working conditions and requires a full examination of the working-places, for, as a rule, the price-lists are not inclusive but contain allowances, that is to say the hewer is not given a flat rate of so much for every ton of coal raised but can claim in addition certain allowances should he, in the course of his work, meet with certain natural obstacles necessitating the doing of work other than the getting of coal. Thus, for example, the price-list may be as follows:[1]—

PRICE LIST

Cutting Large Coal	per ton	2	3
Allowance for Cleaning Coal	,,	0	4½

The 4½d. per ton allowed for cleaning coal to be paid only when the present exceptional section of the seam exists.

Through and Through Coal, the 4½d. per ton for cleaning included	per ton	1	9
Clod[2] scale 0 to 4 inches ..		nil	
,, 4 to 7 ,,	per ton	0	1½
,, 7 to 10 ,,	,,	0	2¼
,, 10 to 13 ,,		0	3
,, 13 to 16 ,,		0	3¾
,, 16 to 19 ,,	,,	0	4½

[1] It is to be understood that price lists vary seam by seam and colliery by colliery, according to district and working conditions.

[2] i.e. dirt between seams.

WAGES AND DISPUTES

The clod between the Top Coal and Middle Coal only to be measured and paid for on above scale.

The clod to be measured at road end and each side of working-place, and average thickness paid for.

Headings .. .. .. per yard	3	8¼
,, (Two Shifts) .. ,,	4	8¼
,, (Three Shifts) .. ,,	5	8¼

When three turns are required to work in a place on any shift, an allowance of 9d. per yard to be paid.

Airways .. .. .. per yard	3	8¼
,, (Double Shift) .. ,,	3	7·87

For every additional five yards driven above the first 10 yards, an allowance of 9d. per yard to be paid.

Cutting Rib in Stall where necessary .. .. .. per yard	1	6
Timbering, 9 feet .. .. per pair	2	4·65
Timbering, any lengths between 6 feet 6 inches and 9 feet .. ,,	2	0
Timbering, up to 6 feet 6 inches ,,	1	7½
Flats .. .. each	1	3·37
Road Posts in Headings only ,,	0	7½
Cogs in Headings and Stalls ,,	1	3·37
Cutting Bottom, up to 15 inches per yard	0	7½
Cutting Bottom, any thickness over 15 inches	·	3
Cutting Top, first lift of Coal in Headings	0	9
Cutting Top, second lift of Coal in Headings .. .. ,,	1	6

The first ripping in stall roads, together with all necessary timber, is included in tonnage price, with the exception of the cogs, which are to be paid for. Should at any time the stall roads require to be ripped a second time, the following prices to be paid. This clause only to apply where there is a coal roof.

			s.	d.
Arching, second lift of Coal Top in Stalls	per yard		0	9
Cutting Coal Top, second lift to the Clift in Stalls			.	3·75
Ripping Clift Top in Headings and Stalls where required per inch thick	,,		0	1½

When the ripping is done back in the road and the rubbish required to be trammed on to the face, an allowance to be paid for tramming as arranged by the Management and the men doing such work.

Where there is abnormal top to contend with, other than ordinary clift, the workmen's wages shall be not less than 7s. 1½d. per shift standard, plus full percentage.[1]

		s.	d.
Drawing Posts	each	0	1½
Drawing Cogs	,,	1	3·37
Partings	,,	3	9
Unloading Rubbish	per tram	0	4½
Making a Tumbling Place	each	3	0
Colliers' Daywork	per day	6	0
Turning Stalls	each	10	6

Four yards of bottom has to be cut and two flats put up in the above price for turning stalls.

In the event of two roads being turned from a Stall road, heading price to be paid from the second road provided it is driven the same dimensions as the other Headings in the District.

The arrangement as to gobbing stalls and any other question that may arise respecting gobbing to be the same as at X colliery, which is equivalent to 3¾d. per day per man.

If a workman loses three days on his own accord in any one week, no gobbing will be paid for that week.

---

[1] This brings into operation the standard and percentages already described.

WAGES AND DISPUTES

When colliers meet with soft coal, faults, rolls, or other unusual conditions, and give notice of same to the Management, the Management and the Colliers affected shall endeavour to arrive at a settlement by which an allowance or extra sum shall be paid, but failing an agreement the Colliers shall be paid not less than 7s. 1½d. per shift on the 1915 standard. If the Management is dissatisfied with the workman after warning has been given, he shall have the right to remove him to another place in a normal condition.

Occasionally inclusive price lists, in which is included payment for ripping, cogs, timbers, etc., are fixed whereby the worker gets a larger tonnage rate and fewer allowances. Even in the case of inclusive price lists allowances have to be made, either by way of making up to a given sum per day or by payment of an extra amount per ton beyond that stated in the price list. This principle of an inclusive tonnage rate with special rates for abnormal places is, we are convinced, the most satisfactory method of calculating piece rates and it is to be regretted that it is not more generally applied.

It is evident that many disputes can arise out of these methods of calculating piece rates, methods which are due in a large measure to the nature of the work done and the extraordinary diversity of the conditions under which the same man must work. Thus, for example, a hewer who is working on a thick coal seam may be getting a large quantity of coal per day one week and the next week he may run into a fault which renders the getting of coal practically or entirely impossible.

The Coal Mines (Minimum Wage) Act, 1912, was intended partly to meet such a case as that last mentioned and generally to secure for all workers underground a decent standard of life by assuring them a minimum daily rate of pay. The quantum of this minimum wage had to be fixed class by class[1] and district by district, by Joint District Boards. The machinery employed was similar to that established by the Trade Boards Act, 1909. For a Joint District Board to be approved as suitable for this purpose it was necessary to show that the Board fairly and adequately represented the workmen in coal mines in the district, and the employers of those workmen, and that the chairman was an independent person appointed by agreement between the two sides or, in default of agreement, by the Board of Trade.

At any time after the minimum rate had been settled the Joint District Board has power to vary such minimum rate : (*a*) at any time by agreement or (*b*) in default of agreement after one year has elapsed since the rate or rates were last settled or varied, on an application made (with three months' notice given after the expiration of the year) by any body of workers or employers, which appears to the Joint District Board to represent any con-

---

[1] Aged and disabled workmen might be excluded from the classes to which the minimum wage applied.

WAGES AND DISPUTES 175

siderable body of opinion amongst either the workmen or the employers concerned.

For the purpose of this Act, Great Britain was divided up into specified districts which districts are not precisely the same as either the Home Office Divisions or the Conciliation Board districts, or the Mining Association or Miners' Federation Districts. The idea was doubtless to divide the coalfields in such a way that the economic conditions of the collieries in each Minimum Wage district were as far as possible the same. To give an example, it would be manifestly impossible to settle the same minimum wage for the Forest of Dean, where the natural conditions and the economic conditions are adverse, as for South Wales where they are favourable.[1]

As a result of the Coal Mines' (Minimum Wage) Act, we therefore see that every underground worker is assured of such minimum wage as the representative Joint District Board of his district considers suitable for his class.

It will, of course, be understood that the minimum wage only comes into operation where

---

[1] The Minimum Wage districts are as follows : Northumberland, Durham, Cumberland, Lancashire and Cheshire, South Yorkshire, West Yorkshire, Cleveland, Derbyshire (exclusive of South Derbyshire), South Derbyshire, Nottinghamshire, Leicestershire, Shropshire, North Staffordshire, South Stafford (exclusive of Cannock Chase) and East Worcestershire, Cannock Chase, Warwickshire, Forest of Dean, Bristol, Somerset, North Wales, South Wales, including Monmouth, the mainland of Scotland. Since the Act of 1912 was passed the Kent coalfield has come into existence.

the getting
possible.

The Coal (Minimum Wage) ...was intended partly to meet such a ... last mentioned and generally to sec... workers underground a decent standa... ...suring them a minimum daily rate o... ...ration of this minimum wage had ... ...seam by seam' and district by distri... ...District Boards. The machinery em... ...milar to that established ... Tr... ...ct. 1909. B... ...pproved as ... this purp... ...essary to show that the Board ... ...dequately represented the workmen i... ...the district, and the employers of ... ...em, and that the chairman was an ... ...erson appointed by agreement betw... ...des or, in default of agreement, by t... Trade.

At ... minimum ra... ...re ... has p...

WAGES AND DISPUTES

siderable body of opinion amongst either the men or the employers concerned.

For the purpose of this Act, Great Britain is divided up into specified districts which are not precisely the same as either the Office Divisions or the Conciliation Board or the Mining Association of Great Britain Districts. The idea was doubtless to divide coalfields in such a way that the natural conditions of the collieries in each Minimum district were as far as possible the same. To take an example, it would be manifestly unfair to settle the same minimum wage for Durham as Dean, where the natural conditions and economic conditions are adverse, as for those where they are favourable.

As a result of the Coal Mines Minimum Act, we therefore see that every underground worker is assured of such minimum as the wage under the standard plus percentages for the district is less than the minimum fixed. Thus, if the 1915 standard plus 23½ per cent plus 18 per cent enables a man to earn less in a day than a man of his class would receive under the Minimum Wage award for his district, such man instead of receiving his piece-rate earnings would claim the minimum wage. He would thus cease to be a piece-worker and would " go upon the minimum." It follows that if piece rates are cut too low there is a temptation on the part of the men to abandon the attempt to make a living by over-exertion and to take things easy and " go upon the minimum." It is generally agreed that the lowest productivity is to be found in those districts where the largest number of men are receiving the minimum wage, and any cutting of rates which has the result of causing the majority of the workers to be thrown on to the minimum is most certainly to be deprecated. It is the cause of much unrest, ill-feeling and slacking. Slacking indeed is bound to occur in this industry, where constant supervision is impossible, and in circumstances where the man gets precisely the same wage whether he works or not so long as he is supposed to be working and is in his working place. The remedy is to be found, in our opinion, by fixing generous, inclusive piece rates whereby a man who works hard and produces a large quantity of coal earns very high wages.

It will be seen from what we have said that

WAGES AND DISPUTES

disputes can readily arise from the following matters relating to wages :—

1. The fixing of day rates.
2. Price lists, allowances, the existence or non-existence of abnormal places, etc.
3. Standard bases and percentages.
4. Minimum rates.
5. Questions relating to war wage; whether payable or not, etc.

In addition to disputes over wages there are to be found many debatable points in respect of working conditions, hours of labour, meal times, stops and the hundred and one questions which arise in all industries between capital and labour.

The coal-mining industry has, however, been organized better than any other to deal with such questions. The negotiating machinery is wellnigh perfect and should be capable, with good will on both sides, of settling any point which can arise. Against the lightning strike the Conciliation Board machinery is, of course, useless. Any conceivable method which might be employed would be, for the lightning strike precludes the possibility of negotiating. Such strikes are not countenanced by the responsible miners' leaders.

The Conciliation Boards to which we have frequently referred are the most important part of this negotiating machinery. They existed in some districts before the passing of the Conciliation Act of 1896, but the purpose of that Act was to regularize the proceedings and encourage the extension of the system. The 1896 Act gives to the Board of Trade[1] certain powers of negotiation and arbitration in case of labour disputes. Its application was not limited to the coal-mining industry.

The Act provided for the registration of such Boards or of new Boards which might in future be established, and required the Boards to furnish such reports of proceedings and other documents as the Board of Trade might reasonably require.

By Sect. 2 of the Act of 1896 it was provided that—

1. " Where a difference exists or is apprehended between an employer, or any class of employers, and workmen, or between different classes of workmen, the Board of Trade may, if they think fit, exercise all or any of the following powers, namely,—

  (a) inquire into the causes and circumstances of the difference ;
  (b) take such steps as to the Board may seem expedient for the purpose of enabling the parties to the difference to meet together, by themselves or their representatives, under the presidency of a chairman mutually agreed upon or nominated by the Board of Trade or by some other person or body, with a view to the amicable settlement of the difference ;
  (c) on the application of employers or workmen interested, and after taking into consideration the existence and adequacy of means available for conciliation in the district or trade and the circumstances of the case,

[1] Such powers are now vested in the Ministry of Labour by the New Ministries and Secretaries Act, 1916.

appoint a person or persons to act as conciliator or as a board of conciliation;

(d) on the application of both parties to the difference, appoint an arbitrator.

2. If any person is so appointed to act as conciliator, he shall inquire into the causes and circumstances of the difference by communication with the parties, and otherwise shall endeavour to bring about a settlement of the difference, and shall report his proceedings to the Board of Trade.

3. If a settlement of the difference is effected either by conciliation or by arbitration, a memorandum of the terms thereof shall be drawn up and signed by the parties or their representatives, and a copy thereof shall be delivered to and kept by the Board of Trade."

Section 4 of the same Act gives power to the Board of Trade to aid in establishing Conciliation Boards. At present such Boards, or Joint District Boards, exercising similar functions, exist in all the coalfields. The New Ministries and Secretaries Act, 1916, and the Coal Mines Agreement (Confirmation) Act, 1917, create the Ministry of Labour and the Coal Control respectively, and give to those departments certain powers of interference in labour disputes. Broadly speaking, it may be said that so far as the coal-mining industry is concerned the Ministry of Labour has the power to appoint arbitrators to decide points which both sides desire shall be arbitrated upon, the Coal Control has power, under the Defence of the Realm

Acts, to issue instructions relative to the management and uses of miners and to act in a negotiating or conciliatory capacity in all disputes between the owners and the workmen subject to this that the Coal Control does not interfere until local machinery has been exhausted, and it does not negotiate while men are on strike, it being its established practice to negotiate in an atmosphere of reason and not of force.

The local machinery above mentioned varies slightly district by district, but in the main the same course is pursued in each coalfield.

The channels through which a dispute passes are as follows :—

Ordinary Dispute at a Colliery

(1) Colliery manager—lodge secretary or committee.
(2) Colliery agent—miners' agent.
(3) District conciliation board representative of the district coal owners and the district miners.
(4) Where negotiation or conciliation is desired the Coal Control Acts, or,
(4a) Where arbitration is desired an arbitrator is appointed by the Ministry of Labour.

District Dispute

(1) District Conciliation Board.
(2) and (2a) as above (4) and (4a).

Minimum Wage Dispute

(1) Joint District Board.

Disputes arising out of minimum wage disputes

have been the subject of conciliation by the Coal Control, but that Department does not interfere with the findings of the proper authority, viz. the Joint District Board.

So far we have treated the matter as though the Miners' Federation of Great Britain was the only Trade Union concerned. This, of course, is not so, and we have only chosen that union because it is the largest and the most developed so far as internal organization is concerned. There are, in fact, many other unions of which the most important are the Firemen Examiners and Deputies, the General Council of Mine Workers other than Miners, and the Colliery Enginemen and Surface Craftsmen Organization, while there is a tendency now apparent for the official classes, the Undermanagers and Managers to combine.

It would seem that no adequate reason exists why all questions should not be peaceably and amicably arranged by negotiation, and it is probable that were an accommodating and friendly spirit present many of the disputes which have arisen in the past would have been so settled. We are of the opinion that much of the bitterness which has characterized the frequent quarrels that have arisen have been due to excusable ignorance on the part of the men and to a failure to disclose the facts on the part of the owners. It is beyond question that a full disclosure of the financial position of colliery concerns to the representatives of the workers engaged in those concerns would do much to convince the men that the employers are not, in many instances, employing bluff to defeat their just aspirations. It would also be salutary if bluff, when it was employed, was proved definitely and clearly to be what it is. Such proof, however, will never be forthcoming until the cards are placed on the table and the workers are in a position to judge for themselves how financial matters stand. It would not perhaps be desirable in the interests of the industry for the financial position of individual concerns to be published broadcast, for in many cases this would disclose a position so verging on bankruptcy as to destroy the credit of the concern and prevent its being carried on at all. We speak of an era when the present system of control has come to an end. But we certainly endorse the statements made in clause xlviii of Sir Arthur Duckham's Report, viz. : "It is essential that there should be complete publicity as to the operations and financial results of the coal industry. The Ministry of Mines should be expressly charged with the duty of publishing, not less than once a year, figures showing the cost of getting coal in each of the districts of the country, and the proportion chargeable to materials, wages, general expenses, interest, profit, and other general items." Such information, we think, would greatly reduce the number of stoppages over wage claims, for if the claim was unreasonable the men could be convincingly answered and if it was reasonable the employers would be unable to argue the case.

That such disclosures would do something towards bringing about industrial peace we have no doubt; that it would abolish industrial war we do not believe. An entire change of heart and attitude is necessary before such a consummation is to be hoped for. So long as capital regards labour as a purchasable commodity and insists on disregarding the human element there will be strife. The time has long gone by when men will consent to be treated as machines. In the majority of cases we believe that the employers recognize this fact, but in some cases they do not. But though every coal owner were an enlightened humanitarian, strikes would still continue unless the men on their side recognized that so long as Capital and Labour draw jointly the chariot of Industry it is necessary for each to help the other. Failure to recognize these facts has already cost the community dear and threatens grave injury to the Commonwealth. The time cannot be far distant when the people will begin to see in industrial warfare evils hardly less grave than those presented by international warfare. It remains to be seen which of the two horses the people will find it necessary to curb or necessary to drive. In the words of the Prime Minister :[1] " With production we get prosperity; without it, we starve. To ensure production, the good will of all engaged in the task of production is essential. With that good will every reasonable cause of complaint must be removed. Confidence must be restored—the confidence of the workman in his employer—yea, the confidence of the employer in the workman,

[1] Parliamentary Debates, Vol. 119, 18th Aug., 1919, col. 1309.

and the confidence of both. Then their business will be conducted under conditions of fairness. That is our problem, and there is the solution."

It is indeed no flight of fancy to see the prospect of actual starvation before us unless productivity increases. Mr. Hoover has warned us that " unless productivity can be rapidly increased there can be nothing but political, moral and economic chaos, finally interpreting itself in loss of life on a scale hitherto undreamed of. No economic policy will bring food to men's stomachs or fuel to their hearths that does not secure the maximum production. There is no use for tears over rising prices; they are to a great degree a visualization of insufficient production."

We live to-day in a country which has just fought a long and bitter war, involving the spending of hundreds of thousands of lives and of thousands of millions of pounds. We are poor. Economy is most urgently needed, not only in Government Offices but also in every home. Purchases should be restricted to bare necessities. Yet on every hand one sees signs of the most lavish expenditure. Under such circumstances supply cannot equal demand for many years. We shall continue with soaring prices to live in a sea of fictitious prosperity until a time comes when the hard facts have to be faced that we are not prosperous, but poor; that the world is poor; and that it is the duty of all to make up for the ravages of war by work—hard, continuous work. We have won Liberty, it remains for us now to win Content.

INDEX

Absenteeism, 82
Accidents, notice of, 36 ; number of in 1851, 38
Acts affecting mines: 1736 (Firing Mines), 16 ; 1775 (Scotland), 14–15 , 1842 (Lord Ashley's), 3, 18, 30–2, 42 ; 1850 (Inspection), 32, 33, 36–8, 41, 42 ; 1855 (Inspection and Regulation), 32, 36, 38–9, 40, 41, 42 ; 1860 (1855 Act revised), 42, 44, 45, 47 ; 1862 (Amending), 42–3 ; 1872 (Consolidation), 46–7, 48, 49 ; 1887 (Regulation), 48, 49 ; 1908 (Eight Hours), 49, 168 ; 1911 (Regulation), 48, 49, 54–5 , 1912 (Minimum Wage), 49, 164, 174, 175 ; 1917 (Agreement Confirmation), 179
Adit, 5 ; ventilating, 12
After-damp, 10, 11
Age-limit, before 1842, 19, 20, 25 ; fixed by Ashley Act, 31 ; raised in 1860, 42 ; why raising opposed, 46
Air-doors, etc., 13, 38, 57, 68
Air-gates worked by children, 22, 24
Airways, driving, 171
American export advantages, 128, 131–2 ; average coal prices, 1913 and 1918, 128–9 ; these compared with British, 129–31
— mines, rise in output, 90–1, 112
Apprenticeship under butty system, 25–6 ; defended in Parliament, 30 ; modified by Ashley Act, 31
Argentine coalfield, 131 (note) ; wheat for coal, 137
Australian State mines, 102–4, 116

Beading, 66
Belgian objection to State mines, 101–2, 117
Belgium, 12 ; her coalfields damaged by war, 121 ; compensated in kind by Germany, 123, 124
Bell pits, 4–5
Board of Trade and disputes, 178, 179 ; powers transferred to Ministry of Labour, 178 (note)
Bord and pillar mining, 4, 66–7
Boys in mines, 19–20, 25, 26, 30, 31, 42, 60, 72, 146
Brattice-cloths, 68
British coal industry, modern status of, 2
Buddle, 43

Butty system, 21 ; apprenticeships under, 25–6 ; responsible for many evils, 26 ; how worked, 26–8 ; wages rates under, 28–9 ; modified by Ashley Act, 31–2

Canals, 147
Capital and labour—reconciliation schemes, 94–8, 99 ; mutual help necessary, 183
Carbon monoxide and dioxide, 10, 11
Certification of managers opposed, 46 ; conceded, 47–8 ; its revolutionary effect, 48–9
Cheshire, 18
Child labour underground, 17 ; abolished, 18, 30 , hours and wages, 19 ; conditions, 19–20 ; ages, 20 ; proportion to adult labour, 20–1 ; how used, 22–4 ; apprenticeship under butty system, 25–6, 30 ; age minimum raised, 42
Choke damp, 11
Clearance at shaft top, 69 ; important to output, 83 ; neglected during war, 83 ; essentials to, 84–5   [–63
Coal Conservation Committee, 1917, 159
— Control, 179, 180, 181
— cutting machine, 61 ; in increasing use, 85 ; number and output, 1903–18, 86
— early industrial use, 3 ; household use, 3
— getting, modern, 60–1 ; a mystery trade, 72
— Industry Commission, 74 ; proposals of employers, 95–7, 98 ; Mining Associations' scheme, 97 ; Sir Arthur Duckham's scheme, 98, 99 , evidence respecting price, 145–7 ; wage increase recommended, 168
— Trade Association, Northumberland and Durham, 41
Collier, modern, 61 ; his training, 71–2 ; day-wage, 172
Collieries, number of, 37 ; financial position of, 181–2
Commissioners of 1854, 34   [22, 30
— report of, on Children in Mines, 18–21,
— South African, on State omnipotence, 100–1
Committee on Accidents in Mines (1835), 22, 43

Conciliation Act, 1896, 177, 178
— Boards, 96, 97, 165, 166, 167, 175, 176, 177, 179, 180, 181
Contracts, 15, 21
Co-operative working, 95
— distribution in 1918, 147
Coroner's records, 35
Cost of living and coal export, 137, 142 ; sent up by dearer coal, 151

Davy lamp and eye disease, 13
Dead work, 83 ; restricted during war, 84
Dean, Forest of, 3, 175
Depth of mines, 4, 55
Deputies, 63
Disputes, time lost in, 78-9, 81 ; often result in strikes, 164 ; wage causes and others, 164, 173-4, 177 ; machinery for negotiating, 177-80
Distribution costs, 1918, 146-7
District Councils, proposed, 96
Drainage, 4 ; adit system of, 5-6
Duckham, Sir Arthur, favours workmen directors, 97 ; his reconciliation scheme, 98, 99 ; advocates publishing costs of coal-getting, 182-3

Earnings per person, 1899-1918, 89-90
Education, wanting in early mine managers, 27, 34 , an aim of miners, 41, 44 ; opposition to, 46   [160
Electric motor power the most economic, — plant, 56
— Power Supply Committee, 163
— Power Supply Scheme, economic advantages of, 161-3
— super-power stations and coal economy, 81-2, 161-3
Engineers, mining, 4
Establishment charges, 146
European coal market and German competition, 127, 130-1
Examination, 63-4
Examiners, 63
Excess Profit Duty, 52
Explosions, 4, 7, 8, 9, 10, 11-12, 35
Export, a matter of c.i.f., 121 , German competition in, 121-7 ; keen American competition, 128-33 ; figures of British, 133 ; improvement doubtful, 134-5, 159 ; danger of high cost and low output, 135 , profits from, in 1918, 138-9 ; kept down home price during war, 140
Export prices, German, 123-4
— trade, 81-2
Expropriation, 135

Factory Acts, 16
Fans, ventilating, 4, 55
Fatfield disaster, 8

Federation of British Industries, effect of dearer coal, 151, 156 ; reactions, 152, 156 ; steel figures as test, 152-6
Feedings stuffs, 146
Felling Colliery, 34
Ferro-manganese, 154
Fire-damp, 4, 7, 8, 9-10, 64   [61, 63
Fireman, the first, 7 ; the modern, 8,
Firing a mine, 16
France, coalfields of, 121, 122 ; compensated by Saar coalfield, 122-3, 124 ; American competition, 130
Frederick the Great, 104
Freights, a British stand-by, 128 ; cheap, advantage of, 130, 131, 133 ; return, economy of, 137-8 ; compared with railway rates, 147-8
Furnaces, ventilating, 12-13

Gases, 8, 9, 10, 11
German rings, 121
— State mines, 101 ; origin, 104 ; analysis of results, 1880-1912, 104-7 , comparison with private mines, 107-110 ; and with German and British ditto, 112 ; extension of, 114
Germany's Treaty obligations, 122-4 ; effect on pre-war output, 124, 126 ; diminished output, 125-6
Getters, 169
Girls in mines, 19, 20, 23-4, 30, 31
Gobbing, 172
Gob fires, 10, 11, 58, 64
" Going on the minimum," 176

Harigild money, 15   [and pony, 60
Haulage, mechanical, 56, 59-60 , hand
— roads, 23, 58, 59, 64-5, 66, 82
Hewers, 18, 21, 169 , price-list of, 170-3
Holidays, time lost through, 74-5, 80
Holing, 61
Holland, State mines of, 104, 117
Home consumer, 142, 143, 144
Horse-keepers, 18
Horses, 146
Hours, early Victorian, 18-19   [143
Household Fuel and Lighting Orders,

Idle mines, 64, 78
Import necessary, 136
Industrial war, cause of, 183
Industry and cost of coal, 151-2, 152-6
Ingot moulds, 154
Inquests, 35
Inspection of Mines Act, 32, 36 ; need for, 34, 35-6 ; amplified, 36, 38
Inspector of Mines, 31 ; powers extended, 36-8   [40
Institute of Mining Engineers, Northern,
Intensity of work, 82, 88-90 , American figures, 90-1 ; cause of decline, 91
Italy, German coal for, 123, 124, 126, 127 ; American competition, 130

INDEX

Joint District Boards, 174–5, 180, 181
— Industrial National Council, 97

Kuhr, 101

Labour in mines, 3; division of, 8 (note); "remarkably pleasant and cheerful," 30
Labour v. Capital, 93–4, 97, 98, 182, 183
Lamps, electric v. oil, 55
Lancashire, 18, 21, 22
Lightning strikes, 177
Loaders, 146
Longwall mining, 4, 60–6
Loss of time through absenteeism, 82, holidays, 74–5, 80; lack of intensity, 88–92, 176; "other causes," 79–80, 81; strikes, 78–9, 81; transport difficulties, 75–8; war causes, 82–3, 134
Loss of trade, 80, 81–2

Management, 2; burden of, 92; improved v. decline in productivity, 93; future, 93–4
Managers, 28; unqualified, 33–4; certification of, 46, 47–8
Matches, etc., forbidden in mines, 54–5
Methane, or fire-damp, 9–10
Midland Mining Commission Report, 22, 25, 26
Mine development, British, 1889–1918, 111; German, 112
Miner, 14; contract systems, 15; freedom of contract, 15–16; eighteenth century, 16–17, wages, 18; hours, 18–19, how employed in 1842, 22, 23; present standard of living, 157; status of, 159
Mine-owners, under butty system, 21, 26, 27–8, 34; inspection, 37; empowered to make rules, 39; promote Act of 1855, 41; criticized, 50–1; surrendered excess profits, 52, provision for demobilized employees, 52–3, 87–8; in conflict with men, 91, 93–4; proposals for reconciliation, 94–6, 158, 181–3
Miners, patriotic, 53; increased productivity of, 157; agreement of with owners, 158, 182, 183
Miners' Federation, 41–2, 175, 181
— Unions, 181
Minimum Wage, 174–6; a cause of low productivity, 176
— districts, 175
Mining Association of Great Britain, 97, 175
Ministry of Labour, 178 note, 179, 180

National Council, proposed, 96

Nationalization of Mines, 98; Belgian opinion, 101–2; German form of, 113–14; failure of, 115–19
Newcomen, 7
New Zealand State mines, 102–3; labour difficulty, 103
Nystagmus, 13

Oldbury explosion, 35
Outcrop, 4, 5
Output, analysed, 74–92
— per man in Britain, 88–9; in America, 90–1; cause of British decline, 91–2, comparison of under State and private ownership, 101, 107–110, 112; not constant in Britain, 112–3; comparison of, against German State ownership, 113; effect of reduced working day, 134–5; need for recovery, 135, 141, 157–8, 184

Pickers, 69
Piece-rates, differential, 165, adjusted to shorter hours, 168; determined by tonnage, or area, 169–70; examples of, 170–3; calculations of, disputes, 173–6
Piece-work, 164, 169, 170–3
Pig-iron, 153
Pit Committees, proposed, 95–6
Ponies, 23, 60
Power, 160
Price of coal, 136–7
— pit-head, 1899–1918, 89–90; steadily rising, 144; Durham scale of 1877, 144; Derby coal, rise, 1914, 1918, 1919, 145; analysis for 1918, 148–9
— to home consumer, 145–7; rise explained, 149–50; effect of rise, 151, 156
Prices f.o.b. for 1907 compared, 132; dependence of an output, 141
Production, Premier's appeal for, 184
Productivity (see Output)
Profits, limited during war, 52
— on exported coal, 1918, 138–9; on home consumption, 140, of merchant, 1914 and 1918, 145, 147; at pit-head, 1918, 148
Promotion disturbed by war, 87–8
Prussian State mines, 104, 105
Pump, wheel and bucket, 6; Savery's, 6, Newcomen's, 7; electric, 56
Pumping, 4; development of, 6–7; modern, 56
Putters, 18, 61, 169

Queensland State Mines, 103–4

Rails, colliery, 85 [147–8
Railway rates during war, 146; in 1918,
— waggons, shortage of, 76–7
Rationing coal justified, 143–4
Rawmarsh, 38

188 BRITISH COAL INDUSTRY

Regulation of mines, 36, 38-9
Ripping, 65, 83, 171, 172
Roads, neglected, 147
Rolling stock, railway, importance of, 76, 77-8, 81 ; colliery, shortage, 84-5
Roof, settling of, 62-5
Royalties, 1918, 148
Rubbish, 172

Saar State mines, 101, 104, 107 ; coalfields, 122, 124, 127
Safety-lamp, 10, 11-12, 13
Salters, 3
Sankey or British scheme of nationalization, 116, 118-19
— wage increase, 168, 169
School of Mines, 40
Scotland, 3, 14, 15, 20, 21, 22
Screening, 69-70
Senghenydd disaster, 11
Shaft bottom, 56-7, 58
Shafts, two, made compulsory, 42-3 ; up-cast and down-cast, 55
Shortage of German coal in 1919, 125-6, of British in 1915, 145 (note)
Signalling, 39
Slacking caused by minimum wage, 176
Sliding scale, 164, 165, 166
South African State Mining Commissioners of 1917, 100, 117
— — Labour Party and Nationalization, 101
South Atlantic trade, 131 ; cost of meeting it, 131-2 ; position, 133
Stalls, 60
Standard of life, miner's, 157 ; to raise, the aim of the Trade Unions, 164
State Mines, German, 101, 104-116, 117-8, Colonial, 102-4, 116 ; Dutch, 104, 117
— ownership problem, 93
Steam boilers, 39
— pump, 6-7
Steel, made dearer by dearer coal, 151, 152-6 ; war shortage of, 85
Stoneman, 65, 170
Strikes, 15-16, 41-2, 77-8, 133, 169 ; time lost through, 78-9
Submarines hinder coal transport, 76 ; proved the need for import, 136
Subsidences, 4
Subsidized export, 136 (note)
Sump, 56
Support, 4

Taxation, 101
Technical education, 40-6
Technicality, 2-3
Temperature, 12
Timber, 149
Timbering, 57, 58-9 ; cost of, 62-3, 149 ; allowances for, 171, 172

Tipper, 69
Tonnage for export, 128 ; return to 1914 level uncertain, 134-5 ; subsidizing, 136 (note)
— general basis of piece-rates, 169
Trade Boards Act, 1909, 174
— Unions and improved conditions, 158, 164, 159 ; further achievement, 159 ; of miners, various, 181
Trammers, 21, 61, 169, 172
Trams or tubs, 55, 56, 58, 60, 61
Transport, 75-8, cheap means neglected, 147
Treasury control, 118
Trespass, 4
Trolleymen, 146
Truck Acts, 47
Tub, an expanding, 44-5

Under-manager, 63
Upper Silesian State mines, 104, 106 ; coalfields, 122, 124, 127

Ventilation, 4, 8, 12-13 ; absence of, 35, 38, cheap divided shaft, 43-4 ; modern method, 67-8
Viewers, 28

Wages and costs, 1914-18, 146-7, 148
— increased by Sankey Report, 149 ; reduction undesirable, 157
— regulation of, 164, standard rates, 165, sliding scale, 165-6 ; 1915 standard, 166 ; War Bonus of 1916, 167 ; War Wage, 1917-18, 167-8 ; Sankey increase in, 168-9 ; piece-rates, 169-73 ; minimum, 174-6
— early Victorian, 18, 19 ; low, compelled child labour, 22, 29 ; day's, under butty system, 28-9
Wales, 3, 7, 14, 20, 24, 46, 175
War Bonus, 167
— difficulties affecting output, 82-8
— service, 87 ; cause of decline in output, 88, 134
— Wage, a flat rate, 167, 169 ; its complications, 167-8
Washing coal, economy of, 70-1
Water-gates, 5
Westphalian Coal Syndicate, 121
— State mines, 104, 107
White damp, 11
Whitley Councils, 97
Winding coal, 22, 24
Woman labour, 17, 18, 30 ; hours and wages, 19, 24, proportionate numbers, 20-1 ; how employed, 22, 23 ; necessity of asserted in Parliament, 31, 65   [17
Women war volunteers for the mines,
— as pickers, 69
Working-day, 112-3, 134-5

UNIVERSITY OF CALIFORNIA LIBRARY
BERKELEY

Return to desk from which borrowed.
This book is DUE on the last date stamped below.

NOV 15 1947

IN STACKS

NOV 7 1961

4 Apr'62JE